C-4767 CAREER EXAMINATION SERIES

This is your PASSBOOK for...

Social Work Assistant II, III

Test Preparation Study Guide Questions & Answers

NLC®

NATIONAL LEARNING CORPORATION®

National Learning Corporation

212 Michael Drive, Syosset, NY 11791
(516) 921-8888 • www.passbooks.com
E-mail: info@passbooks.com

PASSBOOK® SERIES

THE *PASSBOOK® SERIES* has been created to prepare applicants and candidates for the ultimate academic battlefield – the examination room.

At some time in our lives, each and every one of us may be required to take an examination – for validation, matriculation, admission, qualification, registration, certification, or licensure.

Based on the assumption that every applicant or candidate has met the basic formal educational standards, has taken the required number of courses, and read the necessary texts, the *PASSBOOK® SERIES* furnishes the one special preparation which may assure passing with confidence, instead of failing with insecurity. Examination questions – together with answers – are furnished as the basic vehicle for study so that the mysteries of the examination and its compounding difficulties may be eliminated or diminished by a sure method.

This book is meant to help you pass your examination provided that you qualify and are serious in your objective.

The entire field is reviewed through the huge store of content information which is succinctly presented through a provocative and challenging approach – the question-and-answer method.

A climate of success is established by furnishing the correct answers at the end of each test.

You soon learn to recognize types of questions, forms of questions, and patterns of questioning. You may even begin to anticipate expected outcomes.

You perceive that many questions are repeated or adapted so that you can gain acute insights, which may enable you to score many sure points.

You learn how to confront new questions, or types of questions, and to attack them confidently and work out the correct answers.

You note objectives and emphases, and recognize pitfalls and dangers, so that you may make positive educational adjustments.

Moreover, you are kept fully informed in relation to new concepts, methods, practices, and directions in the field.

You discover that you are actually taking the examination all the time: you are preparing for the examination by "taking" an examination, not by reading extraneous and/or supererogatory textbooks.

In short, this PASSBOOK®, used directedly, should be an important factor in helping you to pass your test.

SOCIAL WORK ASSISTANT II, III

DUTIES:

As a Social Work Assistant II, you would perform a variety of case management and service coordination activities for an assigned caseload; interview individuals, their families, and/or others to gather background information, prepare case histories, and determine eligibility for services; advocate on behalf of and assist individuals in identifying and obtaining services; work with interdisciplinary treatment teams and participate in the development and implementation of treatment and service plans; coordinate services between agencies, programs, and providers; and follow-up to ensure individuals' needs are met.

As a Social Work Assistant III, you would perform similar duties as a Social Work Assistant II, manage a more complex caseload, and exercise a higher degree of independence. You would perform a variety of case management and service coordination activities for an assigned caseload; interview individuals, their families, and/or others to gather background information, prepare case histories, and determine eligibility for services; advocate on behalf of and assist individuals in identifying and obtaining services; work with interdisciplinary treatment teams and participate in the development and implementation of treatment and service plans; coordinate services between agencies, programs, and providers; and follow-up to ensure individuals' needs are met.

SUBJECT OF EXAMINATION:

The written test is designed to test for knowledge, skills, and/or abilities in such areas as:

1. **Interviewing** - These questions test for knowledge of the principles and practices employed in obtaining information from individuals through structured conversations. These questions require you to apply the principles, practices, and techniques of effective interviewing to hypothetical interviewing situations. Included are questions that present a problem arising from an interviewing situation, and you must choose the most appropriate course of action to take.
2. **Preparing written material** - These questions test for the ability to present information clearly and accurately, and to organize paragraphs logically and comprehensibly. For some questions, you will be given information in two or three sentences followed by four restatements of the information. You must then choose the best version. For other questions, you will be given paragraphs with their sentences out of order. You must then choose, from four suggestions, the best order for the sentences.
3. **Principles and practices of social casework** - These questions test for the knowledge and understanding of principles and practices used to provide casework services. Questions may cover such topics as developmental, mental, physical and social disabilities and/or impairments; assessing client strengths and needs; building and maintaining relationships with clients and their support network; ability to make and advocate for appropriate service referrals; ability to provide advocacy and support; and professional and ethical concerns in casework practice.
4. **Understanding and interpreting written material** - These questions test how well you comprehend written material. You will be provided with brief reading selections and will be asked questions about the selections. All the information required to answer the questions will be presented in the selections; you will not be required to have any special knowledge relating to the subject areas of the selections.

HOW TO TAKE A TEST

I. YOU MUST PASS AN EXAMINATION

A. WHAT EVERY CANDIDATE SHOULD KNOW

Examination applicants often ask us for help in preparing for the written test. What can I study in advance? What kinds of questions will be asked? How will the test be given? How will the papers be graded?

As an applicant for a civil service examination, you may be wondering about some of these things. Our purpose here is to suggest effective methods of advance study and to describe civil service examinations.

Your chances for success on this examination can be increased if you know how to prepare. Those "pre-examination jitters" can be reduced if you know what to expect. You can even experience an adventure in good citizenship if you know why civil service exams are given.

B. WHY ARE CIVIL SERVICE EXAMINATIONS GIVEN?

Civil service examinations are important to you in two ways. As a citizen, you want public jobs filled by employees who know how to do their work. As a job seeker, you want a fair chance to compete for that job on an equal footing with other candidates. The best-known means of accomplishing this two-fold goal is the competitive examination.

Exams are widely publicized throughout the nation. They may be administered for jobs in federal, state, city, municipal, town or village governments or agencies.

Any citizen may apply, with some limitations, such as the age or residence of applicants. Your experience and education may be reviewed to see whether you meet the requirements for the particular examination. When these requirements exist, they are reasonable and applied consistently to all applicants. Thus, a competitive examination may cause you some uneasiness now, but it is your privilege and safeguard.

C. HOW ARE CIVIL SERVICE EXAMS DEVELOPED?

Examinations are carefully written by trained technicians who are specialists in the field known as "psychological measurement," in consultation with recognized authorities in the field of work that the test will cover. These experts recommend the subject matter areas or skills to be tested; only those knowledges or skills important to your success on the job are included. The most reliable books and source materials available are used as references. Together, the experts and technicians judge the difficulty level of the questions.

Test technicians know how to phrase questions so that the problem is clearly stated. Their ethics do not permit "trick" or "catch" questions. Questions may have been tried out on sample groups, or subjected to statistical analysis, to determine their usefulness.

Written tests are often used in combination with performance tests, ratings of training and experience, and oral interviews. All of these measures combine to form the best-known means of finding the right person for the right job.

II. HOW TO PASS THE WRITTEN TEST

A. NATURE OF THE EXAMINATION

To prepare intelligently for civil service examinations, you should know how they differ from school examinations you have taken. In school you were assigned certain definite pages to read or subjects to cover. The examination questions were quite detailed and usually emphasized memory. Civil service exams, on the other hand, try to discover your present ability to perform the duties of a position, plus your potentiality to learn these duties. In other words, a civil service exam attempts to predict how successful you will be. Questions cover such a broad area that they cannot be as minute and detailed as school exam questions.

In the public service similar kinds of work, or positions, are grouped together in one "class." This process is known as *position-classification.* All the positions in a class are paid according to the salary range for that class. One class title covers all of these positions, and they are all tested by the same examination.

B. FOUR BASIC STEPS

1) Study the announcement

How, then, can you know what subjects to study? Our best answer is: "Learn as much as possible about the class of positions for which you've applied." The exam will test the knowledge, skills and abilities needed to do the work.

Your most valuable source of information about the position you want is the official exam announcement. This announcement lists the training and experience qualifications. Check these standards and apply only if you come reasonably close to meeting them.

The brief description of the position in the examination announcement offers some clues to the subjects which will be tested. Think about the job itself. Review the duties in your mind. Can you perform them, or are there some in which you are rusty? Fill in the blank spots in your preparation.

Many jurisdictions preview the written test in the exam announcement by including a section called "Knowledge and Abilities Required," "Scope of the Examination," or some similar heading. Here you will find out specifically what fields will be tested.

2) Review your own background

Once you learn in general what the position is all about, and what you need to know to do the work, ask yourself which subjects you already know fairly well and which need improvement. You may wonder whether to concentrate on improving your strong areas or on building some background in your fields of weakness. When the announcement has specified "some knowledge" or "considerable knowledge," or has used adjectives like "beginning principles of..." or "advanced ... methods," you can get a clue as to the number and difficulty of questions to be asked in any given field. More questions, and hence broader coverage, would be included for those subjects which are more important in the work. Now weigh your strengths and weaknesses against the job requirements and prepare accordingly.

3) Determine the level of the position

Another way to tell how intensively you should prepare is to understand the level of the job for which you are applying. Is it the entering level? In other words, is this the position in which beginners in a field of work are hired? Or is it an intermediate or advanced level? Sometimes this is indicated by such words as "Junior" or "Senior" in the class title. Other jurisdictions use Roman numerals to designate the level – Clerk I, Clerk II, for example. The word "Supervisor" sometimes appears in the title. If the level is not indicated by the title, check the description of duties. Will you be working under very close supervision, or will you have responsibility for independent decisions in this work?

4) Choose appropriate study materials

Now that you know the subjects to be examined and the relative amount of each subject to be covered, you can choose suitable study materials. For beginning level jobs, or even advanced ones, if you have a pronounced weakness in some aspect of your training, read a modern, standard textbook in that field. Be sure it is up to date and has general coverage. Such books are normally available at your library, and the librarian will be glad to help you locate one. For entry-level positions, questions of appropriate difficulty are chosen – neither highly advanced questions, nor those too simple. Such questions require careful thought but not advanced training.

If the position for which you are applying is technical or advanced, you will read more advanced, specialized material. If you are already familiar with the basic principles of your field, elementary textbooks would waste your time. Concentrate on advanced textbooks and technical periodicals. Think through the concepts and review difficult problems in your field.

These are all general sources. You can get more ideas on your own initiative, following these leads. For example, training manuals and publications of the government agency which employs workers in your field can be useful, particularly for technical and professional positions. A letter or visit to the government department involved may result in more specific study suggestions, and certainly will provide you with a more definite idea of the exact nature of the position you are seeking.

III. KINDS OF TESTS

Tests are used for purposes other than measuring knowledge and ability to perform specified duties. For some positions, it is equally important to test ability to make adjustments to new situations or to profit from training. In others, basic mental abilities not dependent on information are essential. Questions which test these things may not appear as pertinent to the duties of the position as those which test for knowledge and information. Yet they are often highly important parts of a fair examination. For very general questions, it is almost impossible to help you direct your study efforts. What we can do is to point out some of the more common of these general abilities needed in public service positions and describe some typical questions.

1) General information

Broad, general information has been found useful for predicting job success in some kinds of work. This is tested in a variety of ways, from vocabulary lists to questions about current events. Basic background in some field of work, such as sociology or economics, may be sampled in a group of questions. Often these are principles which have become familiar to most persons through exposure rather than through formal training. It is difficult to advise you how to study for these questions; being alert to the world around you is our best suggestion.

2) Verbal ability

An example of an ability needed in many positions is verbal or language ability. Verbal ability is, in brief, the ability to use and understand words. Vocabulary and grammar tests are typical measures of this ability. Reading comprehension or paragraph interpretation questions are common in many kinds of civil service tests. You are given a paragraph of written material and asked to find its central meaning.

3) Numerical ability

Number skills can be tested by the familiar arithmetic problem, by checking paired lists of numbers to see which are alike and which are different, or by interpreting charts and graphs. In the latter test, a graph may be printed in the test booklet which you are asked to use as the basis for answering questions.

4) Observation

A popular test for law-enforcement positions is the observation test. A picture is shown to you for several minutes, then taken away. Questions about the picture test your ability to observe both details and larger elements.

5) Following directions

In many positions in the public service, the employee must be able to carry out written instructions dependably and accurately. You may be given a chart with several columns, each column listing a variety of information. The questions require you to carry out directions involving the information given in the chart.

6) Skills and aptitudes

Performance tests effectively measure some manual skills and aptitudes. When the skill is one in which you are trained, such as typing or shorthand, you can practice. These tests are often very much like those given in business school or high school courses. For many of the other skills and aptitudes, however, no short-time preparation can be made. Skills and abilities natural to you or that you have developed throughout your lifetime are being tested.

Many of the general questions just described provide all the data needed to answer the questions and ask you to use your reasoning ability to find the answers. Your best preparation for these tests, as well as for tests of facts and ideas, is to be at your physical and mental best. You, no doubt, have your own methods of getting into an exam-taking mood and keeping "in shape." The next section lists some ideas on this subject.

IV. KINDS OF QUESTIONS

Only rarely is the "essay" question, which you answer in narrative form, used in civil service tests. Civil service tests are usually of the short-answer type. Full instructions for answering these questions will be given to you at the examination. But in case this is your first experience with short-answer questions and separate answer sheets, here is what you need to know:

1) Multiple-choice Questions

Most popular of the short-answer questions is the "multiple choice" or "best answer" question. It can be used, for example, to test for factual knowledge, ability to solve problems or judgment in meeting situations found at work.

A multiple-choice question is normally one of three types—

- It can begin with an incomplete statement followed by several possible endings. You are to find the one ending which *best* completes the statement, although some of the others may not be entirely wrong.
- It can also be a complete statement in the form of a question which is answered by choosing one of the statements listed.

- It can be in the form of a problem – again you select the best answer.

Here is an example of a multiple-choice question with a discussion which should give you some clues as to the method for choosing the right answer:

When an employee has a complaint about his assignment, the action which will *best* help him overcome his difficulty is to
A. discuss his difficulty with his coworkers
B. take the problem to the head of the organization
C. take the problem to the person who gave him the assignment
D. say nothing to anyone about his complaint

In answering this question, you should study each of the choices to find which is best. Consider choice "A" – Certainly an employee may discuss his complaint with fellow employees, but no change or improvement can result, and the complaint remains unresolved. Choice "B" is a poor choice since the head of the organization probably does not know what assignment you have been given, and taking your problem to him is known as "going over the head" of the supervisor. The supervisor, or person who made the assignment, is the person who can clarify it or correct any injustice. Choice "C" is, therefore, correct. To say nothing, as in choice "D," is unwise. Supervisors have and interest in knowing the problems employees are facing, and the employee is seeking a solution to his problem.

2) True/False Questions

The "true/false" or "right/wrong" form of question is sometimes used. Here a complete statement is given. Your job is to decide whether the statement is right or wrong.

SAMPLE: A roaming cell-phone call to a nearby city costs less than a non-roaming call to a distant city.

This statement is wrong, or false, since roaming calls are more expensive.

This is not a complete list of all possible question forms, although most of the others are variations of these common types. You will always get complete directions for answering questions. Be sure you understand *how* to mark your answers – ask questions until you do.

V. RECORDING YOUR ANSWERS

Computer terminals are used more and more today for many different kinds of exams.

For an examination with very few applicants, you may be told to record your answers in the test booklet itself. Separate answer sheets are much more common. If this separate answer sheet is to be scored by machine – and this is often the case – it is highly important that you mark your answers correctly in order to get credit.

An electronic scoring machine is often used in civil service offices because of the speed with which papers can be scored. Machine-scored answer sheets must be marked with a pencil, which will be given to you. This pencil has a high graphite content which responds to the electronic scoring machine. As a matter of fact, stray dots may register as answers, so do not let your pencil rest on the answer sheet while you are pondering the correct answer. Also, if your pencil lead breaks or is otherwise defective, ask for another.

Since the answer sheet will be dropped in a slot in the scoring machine, be careful not to bend the corners or get the paper crumpled.

The answer sheet normally has five vertical columns of numbers, with 30 numbers to a column. These numbers correspond to the question numbers in your test booklet. After each number, going across the page are four or five pairs of dotted lines. These short dotted lines have small letters or numbers above them. The first two pairs may also have a "T" or "F" above the letters. This indicates that the first two pairs only are to be used if the questions are of the true-false type. If the questions are multiple choice, disregard the "T" and "F" and pay attention only to the small letters or numbers.

Answer your questions in the manner of the sample that follows:

32. The largest city in the United States is
    A. Washington, D.C.
    B. New York City
    C. Chicago
    D. Detroit
    E. San Francisco

1) Choose the answer you think is best. (New York City is the largest, so "B" is correct.)
2) Find the row of dotted lines numbered the same as the question you are answering. (Find row number 32)
3) Find the pair of dotted lines corresponding to the answer. (Find the pair of lines under the mark "B.")
4) Make a solid black mark between the dotted lines.

VI. BEFORE THE TEST

Common sense will help you find procedures to follow to get ready for an examination. Too many of us, however, overlook these sensible measures. Indeed, nervousness and fatigue have been found to be the most serious reasons why applicants fail to do their best on civil service tests. Here is a list of reminders:

- Begin your preparation early – Don't wait until the last minute to go scurrying around for books and materials or to find out what the position is all about.
- Prepare continuously – An hour a night for a week is better than an all-night cram session. This has been definitely established. What is more, a night a week for a month will return better dividends than crowding your study into a shorter period of time.
- Locate the place of the exam – You have been sent a notice telling you when and where to report for the examination. If the location is in a different town or otherwise unfamiliar to you, it would be well to inquire the best route and learn something about the building.
- Relax the night before the test – Allow your mind to rest. Do not study at all that night. Plan some mild recreation or diversion; then go to bed early and get a good night's sleep.
- Get up early enough to make a leisurely trip to the place for the test – This way unforeseen events, traffic snarls, unfamiliar buildings, etc. will not upset you.
- Dress comfortably – A written test is not a fashion show. You will be known by number and not by name, so wear something comfortable.

- Leave excess paraphernalia at home – Shopping bags and odd bundles will get in your way. You need bring only the items mentioned in the official notice you received; usually everything you need is provided. Do not bring reference books to the exam. They will only confuse those last minutes and be taken away from you when in the test room.
- Arrive somewhat ahead of time – If because of transportation schedules you must get there very early, bring a newspaper or magazine to take your mind off yourself while waiting.
- Locate the examination room – When you have found the proper room, you will be directed to the seat or part of the room where you will sit. Sometimes you are given a sheet of instructions to read while you are waiting. Do not fill out any forms until you are told to do so; just read them and be prepared.
- Relax and prepare to listen to the instructions
- If you have any physical problem that may keep you from doing your best, be sure to tell the test administrator. If you are sick or in poor health, you really cannot do your best on the exam. You can come back and take the test some other time.

VII. AT THE TEST

The day of the test is here and you have the test booklet in your hand. The temptation to get going is very strong. Caution! There is more to success than knowing the right answers. You must know how to identify your papers and understand variations in the type of short-answer question used in this particular examination. Follow these suggestions for maximum results from your efforts:

1) Cooperate with the monitor

The test administrator has a duty to create a situation in which you can be as much at ease as possible. He will give instructions, tell you when to begin, check to see that you are marking your answer sheet correctly, and so on. He is not there to guard you, although he will see that your competitors do not take unfair advantage. He wants to help you do your best.

2) Listen to all instructions

Don't jump the gun! Wait until you understand all directions. In most civil service tests you get more time than you need to answer the questions. So don't be in a hurry. Read each word of instructions until you clearly understand the meaning. Study the examples, listen to all announcements and follow directions. Ask questions if you do not understand what to do.

3) Identify your papers

Civil service exams are usually identified by number only. You will be assigned a number; you must not put your name on your test papers. Be sure to copy your number correctly. Since more than one exam may be given, copy your exact examination title.

4) Plan your time

Unless you are told that a test is a "speed" or "rate of work" test, speed itself is usually not important. Time enough to answer all the questions will be provided, but this does not mean that you have all day. An overall time limit has been set. Divide the total time (in minutes) by the number of questions to determine the approximate time you have for each question.

5) Do not linger over difficult questions

If you come across a difficult question, mark it with a paper clip (useful to have along) and come back to it when you have been through the booklet. One caution if you do this – be sure to skip a number on your answer sheet as well. Check often to be sure that you have not lost your place and that you are marking in the row numbered the same as the question you are answering.

6) Read the questions

Be sure you know what the question asks! Many capable people are unsuccessful because they failed to *read* the questions correctly.

7) Answer all questions

Unless you have been instructed that a penalty will be deducted for incorrect answers, it is better to guess than to omit a question.

8) Speed tests

It is often better NOT to guess on speed tests. It has been found that on timed tests people are tempted to spend the last few seconds before time is called in marking answers at random – without even reading them – in the hope of picking up a few extra points. To discourage this practice, the instructions may warn you that your score will be "corrected" for guessing. That is, a penalty will be applied. The incorrect answers will be deducted from the correct ones, or some other penalty formula will be used.

9) Review your answers

If you finish before time is called, go back to the questions you guessed or omitted to give them further thought. Review other answers if you have time.

10) Return your test materials

If you are ready to leave before others have finished or time is called, take ALL your materials to the monitor and leave quietly. Never take any test material with you. The monitor can discover whose papers are not complete, and taking a test booklet may be grounds for disqualification.

VIII. EXAMINATION TECHNIQUES

1) Read the general instructions carefully. These are usually printed on the first page of the exam booklet. As a rule, these instructions refer to the timing of the examination; the fact that you should not start work until the signal and must stop work at a signal, etc. If there are any *special* instructions, such as a choice of questions to be answered, make sure that you note this instruction carefully.

2) When you are ready to start work on the examination, that is as soon as the signal has been given, read the instructions to each question booklet, underline any key words or phrases, such as *least, best, outline, describe* and the like. In this way you will tend to answer as requested rather than discover on reviewing your paper that you *listed without describing*, that you selected the *worst* choice rather than the *best* choice, etc.

3) If the examination is of the objective or multiple-choice type – that is, each question will also give a series of possible answers: A, B, C or D, and you are called upon to select the best answer and write the letter next to that answer on your answer paper – it is advisable to start answering each question in turn. There may be anywhere from 50 to 100 such questions in the three or four hours allotted and you can see how much time would be taken if you read through all the questions before beginning to answer any. Furthermore, if you come across a question or group of questions which you know would be difficult to answer, it would undoubtedly affect your handling of all the other questions.

4) If the examination is of the essay type and contains but a few questions, it is a moot point as to whether you should read all the questions before starting to answer any one. Of course, if you are given a choice – say five out of seven and the like – then it is essential to read all the questions so you can eliminate the two that are most difficult. If, however, you are asked to answer all the questions, there may be danger in trying to answer the easiest one first because you may find that you will spend too much time on it. The best technique is to answer the first question, then proceed to the second, etc.

5) Time your answers. Before the exam begins, write down the time it started, then add the time allowed for the examination and write down the time it must be completed, then divide the time available somewhat as follows:
   - If 3-1/2 hours are allowed, that would be 210 minutes. If you have 80 objective-type questions, that would be an average of 2-1/2 minutes per question. Allow yourself no more than 2 minutes per question, or a total of 160 minutes, which will permit about 50 minutes to review.
   - If for the time allotment of 210 minutes there are 7 essay questions to answer, that would average about 30 minutes a question. Give yourself only 25 minutes per question so that you have about 35 minutes to review.

6) The most important instruction is to *read each question* and make sure you know what is wanted. The second most important instruction is to *time yourself properly* so that you answer every question. The third most important instruction is to *answer every question.* Guess if you have to but include something for each question. Remember that you will receive no credit for a blank and will probably receive some credit if you write something in answer to an essay question. If you guess a letter – say "B" for a multiple-choice question – you may have guessed right. If you leave a blank as an answer to a multiple-choice question, the examiners may respect your feelings but it will not add a point to your score. Some exams may penalize you for wrong answers, so in such cases *only*, you may not want to guess unless you have some basis for your answer.

7) Suggestions
   a. Objective-type questions
      1. Examine the question booklet for proper sequence of pages and questions
      2. Read all instructions carefully
      3. Skip any question which seems too difficult; return to it after all other questions have been answered
      4. Apportion your time properly; do not spend too much time on any single question or group of questions

5. Note and underline key words – *all, most, fewest, least, best, worst, same, opposite,* etc.
6. Pay particular attention to negatives
7. Note unusual option, e.g., unduly long, short, complex, different or similar in content to the body of the question
8. Observe the use of "hedging" words – *probably, may, most likely,* etc.
9. Make sure that your answer is put next to the same number as the question
10. Do not second-guess unless you have good reason to believe the second answer is definitely more correct
11. Cross out original answer if you decide another answer is more accurate; do not erase until you are ready to hand your paper in
12. Answer all questions; guess unless instructed otherwise
13. Leave time for review

b. Essay questions
1. Read each question carefully
2. Determine exactly what is wanted. Underline key words or phrases.
3. Decide on outline or paragraph answer
4. Include many different points and elements unless asked to develop any one or two points or elements
5. Show impartiality by giving pros and cons unless directed to select one side only
6. Make and write down any assumptions you find necessary to answer the questions
7. Watch your English, grammar, punctuation and choice of words
8. Time your answers; don't crowd material

8) Answering the essay question

Most essay questions can be answered by framing the specific response around several key words or ideas. Here are a few such key words or ideas:

M's: manpower, materials, methods, money, management
P's: purpose, program, policy, plan, procedure, practice, problems, pitfalls, personnel, public relations

a. Six basic steps in handling problems:
1. Preliminary plan and background development
2. Collect information, data and facts
3. Analyze and interpret information, data and facts
4. Analyze and develop solutions as well as make recommendations
5. Prepare report and sell recommendations
6. Install recommendations and follow up effectiveness

b. Pitfalls to avoid
1. *Taking things for granted* – A statement of the situation does not necessarily imply that each of the elements is necessarily true; for example, a complaint may be invalid and biased so that all that can be taken for granted is that a complaint has been registered

2. *Considering only one side of a situation* – Wherever possible, indicate several alternatives and then point out the reasons you selected the best one
3. *Failing to indicate follow up* – Whenever your answer indicates action on your part, make certain that you will take proper follow-up action to see how successful your recommendations, procedures or actions turn out to be
4. *Taking too long in answering any single question* – Remember to time your answers properly

IX. AFTER THE TEST

Scoring procedures differ in detail among civil service jurisdictions although the general principles are the same. Whether the papers are hand-scored or graded by machine we have described, they are nearly always graded by number. That is, the person who marks the paper knows only the number – never the name – of the applicant. Not until all the papers have been graded will they be matched with names. If other tests, such as training and experience or oral interview ratings have been given, scores will be combined. Different parts of the examination usually have different weights. For example, the written test might count 60 percent of the final grade, and a rating of training and experience 40 percent. In many jurisdictions, veterans will have a certain number of points added to their grades.

After the final grade has been determined, the names are placed in grade order and an eligible list is established. There are various methods for resolving ties between those who get the same final grade – probably the most common is to place first the name of the person whose application was received first. Job offers are made from the eligible list in the order the names appear on it. You will be notified of your grade and your rank as soon as all these computations have been made. This will be done as rapidly as possible.

People who are found to meet the requirements in the announcement are called "eligibles." Their names are put on a list of eligible candidates. An eligible's chances of getting a job depend on how high he stands on this list and how fast agencies are filling jobs from the list.

When a job is to be filled from a list of eligibles, the agency asks for the names of people on the list of eligibles for that job. When the civil service commission receives this request, it sends to the agency the names of the three people highest on this list. Or, if the job to be filled has specialized requirements, the office sends the agency the names of the top three persons who meet these requirements from the general list.

The appointing officer makes a choice from among the three people whose names were sent to him. If the selected person accepts the appointment, the names of the others are put back on the list to be considered for future openings.

That is the rule in hiring from all kinds of eligible lists, whether they are for typist, carpenter, chemist, or something else. For every vacancy, the appointing officer has his choice of any one of the top three eligibles on the list. This explains why the person whose name is on top of the list sometimes does not get an appointment when some of the persons lower on the list do. If the appointing officer chooses the second or third eligible, the No. 1 eligible does not get a job at once, but stays on the list until he is appointed or the list is terminated.

X. HOW TO PASS THE INTERVIEW TEST

The examination for which you applied requires an oral interview test. You have already taken the written test and you are now being called for the interview test – the final part of the formal examination.

You may think that it is not possible to prepare for an interview test and that there are no procedures to follow during an interview. Our purpose is to point out some things you can do in advance that will help you and some good rules to follow and pitfalls to avoid while you are being interviewed.

What is an interview supposed to test?

The written examination is designed to test the technical knowledge and competence of the candidate; the oral is designed to evaluate intangible qualities, not readily measured otherwise, and to establish a list showing the relative fitness of each candidate – as measured against his competitors – for the position sought. Scoring is not on the basis of "right" and "wrong," but on a sliding scale of values ranging from "not passable" to "outstanding." As a matter of fact, it is possible to achieve a relatively low score without a single "incorrect" answer because of evident weakness in the qualities being measured.

Occasionally, an examination may consist entirely of an oral test – either an individual or a group oral. In such cases, information is sought concerning the technical knowledges and abilities of the candidate, since there has been no written examination for this purpose. More commonly, however, an oral test is used to supplement a written examination.

Who conducts interviews?

The composition of oral boards varies among different jurisdictions. In nearly all, a representative of the personnel department serves as chairman. One of the members of the board may be a representative of the department in which the candidate would work. In some cases, "outside experts" are used, and, frequently, a businessman or some other representative of the general public is asked to serve. Labor and management or other special groups may be represented. The aim is to secure the services of experts in the appropriate field.

However the board is composed, it is a good idea (and not at all improper or unethical) to ascertain in advance of the interview who the members are and what groups they represent. When you are introduced to them, you will have some idea of their backgrounds and interests, and at least you will not stutter and stammer over their names.

What should be done before the interview?

While knowledge about the board members is useful and takes some of the surprise element out of the interview, there is other preparation which is more substantive. It *is* possible to prepare for an oral interview – in several ways:

1) Keep a copy of your application and review it carefully before the interview

This may be the only document before the oral board, and the starting point of the interview. Know what education and experience you have listed there, and the sequence and dates of all of it. Sometimes the board will ask you to review the highlights of your experience for them; you should not have to hem and haw doing it.

2) Study the class specification and the examination announcement

Usually, the oral board has one or both of these to guide them. The qualities, characteristics or knowledges required by the position sought are stated in these documents. They offer valuable clues as to the nature of the oral interview. For example, if the job involves supervisory responsibilities, the announcement will usually indicate that knowledge of modern supervisory methods and the qualifications of the candidate as a supervisor will be tested. If so, you can expect such questions, frequently in the form of a hypothetical situation which you are expected to solve. NEVER go into an oral without knowledge of the duties and responsibilities of the job you seek.

3) Think through each qualification required

Try to visualize the kind of questions you would ask if you were a board member. How well could you answer them? Try especially to appraise your own knowledge and background in each area, *measured against the job sought*, and identify any areas in which you are weak. Be critical and realistic – do not flatter yourself.

4) Do some general reading in areas in which you feel you may be weak

For example, if the job involves supervision and your past experience has NOT, some general reading in supervisory methods and practices, particularly in the field of human relations, might be useful. Do NOT study agency procedures or detailed manuals. The oral board will be testing your understanding and capacity, not your memory.

5) Get a good night's sleep and watch your general health and mental attitude

You will want a clear head at the interview. Take care of a cold or any other minor ailment, and of course, no hangovers.

What should be done on the day of the interview?

Now comes the day of the interview itself. Give yourself plenty of time to get there. Plan to arrive somewhat ahead of the scheduled time, particularly if your appointment is in the fore part of the day. If a previous candidate fails to appear, the board might be ready for you a bit early. By early afternoon an oral board is almost invariably behind schedule if there are many candidates, and you may have to wait. Take along a book or magazine to read, or your application to review, but leave any extraneous material in the waiting room when you go in for your interview. In any event, relax and compose yourself.

The matter of dress is important. The board is forming impressions about you – from your experience, your manners, your attitude, and your appearance. Give your personal appearance careful attention. Dress your best, but not your flashiest. Choose conservative, appropriate clothing, and be sure it is immaculate. This is a business interview, and your appearance should indicate that you regard it as such. Besides, being well groomed and properly dressed will help boost your confidence.

Sooner or later, someone will call your name and escort you into the interview room. *This is it.* From here on you are on your own. It is too late for any more preparation. But remember, you asked for this opportunity to prove your fitness, and you are here because your request was granted.

What happens when you go in?

The usual sequence of events will be as follows: The clerk (who is often the board stenographer) will introduce you to the chairman of the oral board, who will introduce you to the other members of the board. Acknowledge the introductions before you sit down. Do not be surprised if you find a microphone facing you or a stenotypist sitting by. Oral interviews are usually recorded in the event of an appeal or other review.

Usually the chairman of the board will open the interview by reviewing the highlights of your education and work experience from your application – primarily for the benefit of the other members of the board, as well as to get the material into the record. Do not interrupt or comment unless there is an error or significant misinterpretation; if that is the case, do not hesitate. But do not quibble about insignificant matters. Also, he will usually ask you some question about your education, experience or your present job – partly to get you to start talking and to establish the interviewing "rapport." He may start the actual questioning, or turn it over to one of the other members. Frequently, each member undertakes the questioning on a particular area, one in which he is perhaps most competent, so you can expect each member to participate in the examination. Because time is limited, you may also expect some rather abrupt switches in the direction the questioning takes, so do not be upset by it. Normally, a board member will not pursue a single line of questioning unless he discovers a particular strength or weakness.

After each member has participated, the chairman will usually ask whether any member has any further questions, then will ask you if you have anything you wish to add. Unless you are expecting this question, it may floor you. Worse, it may start you off on an extended, extemporaneous speech. The board is not usually seeking more information. The question is principally to offer you a last opportunity to present further qualifications or to indicate that you have nothing to add. So, if you feel that a significant qualification or characteristic has been overlooked, it is proper to point it out in a sentence or so. Do not compliment the board on the thoroughness of their examination – they have been sketchy, and you know it. If you wish, merely say, "No thank you, I have nothing further to add." This is a point where you can "talk yourself out" of a good impression or fail to present an important bit of information. Remember, *you close the interview yourself.*

The chairman will then say, "That is all, Mr. ______, thank you." Do not be startled; the interview is over, and quicker than you think. Thank him, gather your belongings and take your leave. Save your sigh of relief for the other side of the door.

How to put your best foot forward

Throughout this entire process, you may feel that the board individually and collectively is trying to pierce your defenses, seek out your hidden weaknesses and embarrass and confuse you. Actually, this is not true. They are obliged to make an appraisal of your qualifications for the job you are seeking, and they want to see you in your best light. Remember, they must interview all candidates and a non-cooperative candidate may become a failure in spite of their best efforts to bring out his qualifications. Here are 15 suggestions that will help you:

1) Be natural – Keep your attitude confident, not cocky

If you are not confident that you can do the job, do not expect the board to be. Do not apologize for your weaknesses, try to bring out your strong points. The board is interested in a positive, not negative, presentation. Cockiness will antagonize any board member and make him wonder if you are covering up a weakness by a false show of strength.

2) Get comfortable, but don't lounge or sprawl

Sit erectly but not stiffly. A careless posture may lead the board to conclude that you are careless in other things, or at least that you are not impressed by the importance of the occasion. Either conclusion is natural, even if incorrect. Do not fuss with your clothing, a pencil or an ashtray. Your hands may occasionally be useful to emphasize a point; do not let them become a point of distraction.

3) Do not wisecrack or make small talk

This is a serious situation, and your attitude should show that you consider it as such. Further, the time of the board is limited – they do not want to waste it, and neither should you.

4) Do not exaggerate your experience or abilities

In the first place, from information in the application or other interviews and sources, the board may know more about you than you think. Secondly, you probably will not get away with it. An experienced board is rather adept at spotting such a situation, so do not take the chance.

5) If you know a board member, do not make a point of it, yet do not hide it

Certainly you are not fooling him, and probably not the other members of the board. Do not try to take advantage of your acquaintanceship – it will probably do you little good.

6) Do not dominate the interview

Let the board do that. They will give you the clues – do not assume that you have to do all the talking. Realize that the board has a number of questions to ask you, and do not try to take up all the interview time by showing off your extensive knowledge of the answer to the first one.

7) Be attentive

You only have 20 minutes or so, and you should keep your attention at its sharpest throughout. When a member is addressing a problem or question to you, give him your undivided attention. Address your reply principally to him, but do not exclude the other board members.

8) Do not interrupt

A board member may be stating a problem for you to analyze. He will ask you a question when the time comes. Let him state the problem, and wait for the question.

9) Make sure you understand the question

Do not try to answer until you are sure what the question is. If it is not clear, restate it in your own words or ask the board member to clarify it for you. However, do not haggle about minor elements.

10) Reply promptly but not hastily

A common entry on oral board rating sheets is "candidate responded readily," or "candidate hesitated in replies." Respond as promptly and quickly as you can, but do not jump to a hasty, ill-considered answer.

11) Do not be peremptory in your answers

A brief answer is proper – but do not fire your answer back. That is a losing game from your point of view. The board member can probably ask questions much faster than you can answer them.

12) Do not try to create the answer you think the board member wants

He is interested in what kind of mind you have and how it works – not in playing games. Furthermore, he can usually spot this practice and will actually grade you down on it.

13) Do not switch sides in your reply merely to agree with a board member

Frequently, a member will take a contrary position merely to draw you out and to see if you are willing and able to defend your point of view. Do not start a debate, yet do not surrender a good position. If a position is worth taking, it is worth defending.

14) Do not be afraid to admit an error in judgment if you are shown to be wrong

The board knows that you are forced to reply without any opportunity for careful consideration. Your answer may be demonstrably wrong. If so, admit it and get on with the interview.

15) Do not dwell at length on your present job

The opening question may relate to your present assignment. Answer the question but do not go into an extended discussion. You are being examined for a *new* job, not your present one. As a matter of fact, try to phrase ALL your answers in terms of the job for which you are being examined.

Basis of Rating

Probably you will forget most of these "do's" and "don'ts" when you walk into the oral interview room. Even remembering them all will not ensure you a passing grade. Perhaps you did not have the qualifications in the first place. But remembering them will help you to put your best foot forward, without treading on the toes of the board members.

Rumor and popular opinion to the contrary notwithstanding, an oral board wants you to make the best appearance possible. They know you are under pressure – but they also want to see how you respond to it as a guide to what your reaction would be under the pressures of the job you seek. They will be influenced by the degree of poise you display, the personal traits you show and the manner in which you respond.

ABOUT THIS BOOK

This book contains tests divided into Examination Sections. Go through each test, answering every question in the margin. We have also attached a sample answer sheet at the back of the book that can be removed and used. At the end of each test look at the answer key and check your answers. On the ones you got wrong, look at the right answer choice and learn. Do not fill in the answers first. Do not memorize the questions and answers, but understand the answer and principles involved. On your test, the questions will likely be different from the samples. Questions are changed and new ones added. If you understand these past questions you should have success with any changes that arise. Tests may consist of several types of questions. We have additional books on each subject should more study be advisable or necessary for you. Finally, the more you study, the better prepared you will be. This book is intended to be the last thing you study before you walk into the examination room. Prior study of relevant texts is also recommended. NLC publishes some of these in our Fundamental Series. Knowledge and good sense are important factors in passing your exam. Good luck also helps. So now study this Passbook, absorb the material contained within and take that knowledge into the examination. Then do your best to pass that exam.

EXAMINATION SECTION

INTERVIEWING

EXAMINATION SECTION

TEST 1

DIRECTIONS: Each question or incomplete statement is followed by several suggested answers or completions. Select the one that BEST answers the question or completes the statement. *PRINT THE LETTER OF THE CORRECT ANSWER IN THE SPACE AT THE RIGHT.*

1. Of the following, the MAIN advantage to the supervisor of using the indirect (or nondirective) interview, in which he asks only guiding questions and encourages the employee to do most of the talking, is that he can 1.____
   A. obtain a mass of information about the employee in a very short period of time
   B. easily get at facts which the employee wishes to conceal
   C. get answers which are not slanted or biased in order to win his favor
   D. effectively deal with an employee's serious emotional problems

2. An interviewer under your supervision routinely closes his interview with a reassuring remark such as, "I'm sure you soon will be well," or "Everything will soon be all right." 2.____
   This practice is USUALLY considered
   A. *advisable*, chiefly because the interviewer may make the patient feel better
   B. *inadvisable*, chiefly because it may cause a patient who is seriously ill to doubt the worker's understanding of the situation
   C. *advisable*, chiefly because the patient becomes more receptive if further interviews are needed
   D. *inadvisable*, chiefly because the interviewer should usually not show that he is emotionally involved

3. An interviewer has just ushered out a client he has interviewed. As the interviewer is preparing to leave, the client mentions a fact that seems to contradict the information he has given. 3.____
   Of the following, it would be BEST for the interviewer at this time to
   A. make no response but write the fact down in his report and plan to come back another day
   B. point out to the client that he has contradicted himself and ask for an explanation
   C. ask the client to elaborate on the comment and attempt to find out further information about the fact
   D. disregard the comment since the client was probably exhausted and not thinking clearly

4. A client who is being interviewed insists on certain facts. The interviewer knows that these statements are incorrect. 4.____
In regard to the rest of the client's statements, the interviewer is MOST justified to
   A. disregard any information the client gives which cannot be verified
   B. try to discover other misstatements by confronting the client with the discrepancy
   C. consider everything else which the client has said as the truth unless proved otherwise
   D. ask the client to prove his statements

5. Immediately after the interviewer identifies himself to a client, she says in a hysterical voice that he is not to be trusted. 5.____
Of the following, the BEST course of action for the interviewer to follow would be to
   A. tell the woman sternly that if she does not stay calm, he will leave
   B. assure the woman that there is no cause to worry
   C. ignore the woman until she becomes quiet
   D. ask the woman to explain her problem

6. Assume that you are an interviewer and that one of your interviewees has asked you for advice on dealing with a personal problem. 6.____
Of the following, the BEST action for you to take is to
   A. tell him about a similar problem which you know worked out well
   B. advise him not to worry
   C. explain that the problem is quite a usual one and that the situation will be brighter soon
   D. give no opinion and change the subject when practicable

7. All of the following are generally good approaches for an interviewer to use in order to improve his interviews EXCEPT 7.____
   A. developing a routine approach so that interviews can be standardized
   B. comparing his procedure with that of others engaged in similar work
   C. reviewing each interview critically, picking out one or two weak points to concentrate on improving
   D. comparing his own more successful and less successful interviews

8. Assume that a supervisor suggests at a staff meeting that digital recorders be provided for interviewers. Following are four arguments *against* the use of digital recorders that are raised by other members of the staff that might be valid: 8.____
   I. Recorded interviews provide too much unnecessary information
   II. Recorded interviews provide no record of manner or gestures
   III. Digital recorders are too cumbersome and difficult for the average supervisor to manage
   IV. Digital recorders may inhibit the interviewee

Which one of the following choices MOST accurately classifies the above into those which are generally *invalid* and those which are *not*?
A. I and II are generally valid, but III and IV are not.
B. IV is generally valid, but I, II, and III are not.
C. I, II, and IV are generally valid, but III is not.
D. I, II, III, and IV are generally valid.

9. During an interview, the PRIMARY advantage of the technique of using questions as opposed to allowing the interviewee to talk freely is that questioning 9.____
A. gives the interviewer greater control
B. provides a more complete picture
C. makes the interviewee more relaxed
D. decreases the opportunity for exaggeration

10. Assume that, in conducting an interview, an interviewer takes into consideration the age, sex, education, and background of the subject. 10.____
This practice is GENERALLY considered
A. *undesirable*, mainly because an interviewer may be prejudiced by such factors
B. *desirable*, mainly because these are factors which might influence a person's response to certain questions
C. *undesirable*, mainly because these factors rarely have any bearing on the matter being investigated
D. *desirable*, mainly because certain categories of people answer certain questions in the same way

11. If a client should begin to tell his life story during an interview, the BEST course of action for an interviewer to take is to 11.____
A. interrupt immediately and insist that they return to business
B. listen attentively until the client finishes and then ask if they can return to the subject
C. pretend to have other business and come back later to see the client
D. interrupt politely at an appropriate point and direct the client's attention to the subject

12. An interviewer who is trying to discover the circumstances surrounding a client's accident would be MOST successful during an interview if he avoided questions which 12.____
A. lead the client to discuss the matter in detail
B. can easily be answered by either "yes" or "no"
C. ask for specific information
D. may be embarrassing or annoying to the client

13. A client being interviewed may develop an emotional reaction (positive or negative) toward the interviewer. 13.____
The BEST attitude for the interviewer to take toward such feelings is that they are
A. *inevitable*; they should be accepted but kept under control
B. *unusual*; they should be treated impersonally

C. *obstructive*; they should be resisted at all costs
D. *abnormal*; they should be eliminated as soon as possible

14. Encouraging the client being interviewed to talk freely at first is a technique that is supported by all of the following reasons EXCEPT that it 14.____
A. tends to counteract any preconceived ideas that the interviewer may have entertained about the client
B. gives the interviewer a chance to learn the best method of approach to obtain additional information
C. inhibits the client from looking to the interviewer for support and advice
D. allows the client to reveal the answers to many questions before they are asked

15. Of the following, generally the MOST effective way for an interviewer to assure full cooperation from the client he is interviewing is to 15.____
A. sympathize with the client's problems and assure him of concern
B. tell a few jokes before beginning to ask questions
C. convince the patient that the answers to the questions will help him as well as the interviewer
D. arrange the interview when the client feels best

16. Since many elderly people are bewildered and helpless when interviewed, special consideration should be given to them. 16.____
Of the following, the BEST way for an interviewer to *initially* approach elderly clients who express anxiety and fear is to
A. assure them that they have nothing to worry about
B. listen patiently and show interest in them
C. point out the specific course of action that is best for them
D. explain to them that many people have overcome much greater difficulties

17. Assume that, in planning an initial interview, an interviewer determines in advance what information is needed in order to fulfill the purpose of the interview. 17.____
Of the following, this procedure usually does NOT
A. reduce the number of additional interviews required
B. expedite the processing of the case
C. improve public opinion of the interviewer's agency
D. assure the cooperation of the person interviewed

18. Sometimes an interviewer deliberately introduces his own personal interests and opinions into an interview with a client. 18.____
In general, this practice should be considered
A. *desirable*, primarily because the relationship between client and interviewer becomes social rather than businesslike
B. *undesirable*, primarily because the client might complain to his supervisor
C. *desirable*, primarily because the focus of attention is directed toward the client
D. *undesirable*, primarily because an argument between client and interviewer could result

19. The one of the following types of interviewees who presents the LEAST difficult problem to handle is the person who 19.____
   A. answers with a great many qualifications
   B. talks at length about unrelated subjects so that the interviewer cannot ask questions
   C. has difficulty understanding the interviewer's vocabulary
   D. breaks into the middle of sentences and completes them with a meaning of his own

20. A man being interviewed is entitled to Medicaid, but he refuses to sign up for it because he says he cannot accept any form of welfare. 20.____
Of the following, the BEST course of action for an interviewer to take FIRST is to
   A. try to discover the reason for his feeling this way
   B. tell him that he should be glad financial help is available
   C. explain that others cannot help him if he will not help himself
   D. suggest that he speak to someone who is already on Medicaid

21. Of the following, the outcome of an interview by an interviewer depend MOST heavily on the 21.____
   A. personality of the interviewee
   B. personality of the interviewer
   C. subject matter of the questions asked
   D. interaction between interviewer and interviewee

22. Some clients being interviewed by an interviewer are primarily interested in making a favorable impression. 22.____
The interviewer should be aware of the fact that such clients are MORE likely than other clients to
   A. try to anticipate the answers the interviewer is looking for
   B. answer all questions openly and frankly
   C. try to assume the role of interviewer
   D. be anxious to get the interview over as quickly as possible

23. The type of interview which a hospital care interviewer usually conducts is *substantially different* from most interviewing situations in all of the following EXCEPT the 23.____
   A. setting
   B. kinds of clients
   C. techniques employed
   D. kinds of problems

24. During an interview, an interviewer uses a "leading question." 24.____
This type of question is so-called because it *generally*
   A. starts a series of questions about one topic
   B. suggests the answer which the interviewer wants
   C. forms the basis for a following "trick" question
   D. sets, at the beginning, the tone of the interview

25. An interviewer may face various difficulties when he tries to obtain information from a client. 25.____
Of the following, the difficulty which is EASIEST for the interviewer to overcome occurs when a client
   A. is unwilling to reveal the information
   B. misunderstands what information is needed
   C. does not have the information available to him
   D. is unable to coherently give the information requested

KEY (CORRECT ANSWERS)

1.	C	11.	D
2.	B	12.	B
3.	C	13.	A
4.	C	14.	C
5.	D	15.	C
6.	D	16.	B
7.	A	17.	D
8.	C	18.	D
9.	A	19.	C
10.	B	20.	A

21.	D
22.	A
23.	C
24.	B
25.	B

TEST 2

DIRECTIONS: Each question or incomplete statement is followed by several suggested answers or completions. Select the one that BEST answers the question or completes the statement. *PRINT THE LETTER OF THE CORRECT ANSWER IN THE SPACE AT THE RIGHT.*

1. Of the following, the MOST appropriate manner for an interviewer to assume during an interview with a client is 1.____
   A. authoritarian B. paternal C. casual D. businesslike

2. The systematic study of interviewing theory, principles, and techniques by an interviewer will USUALLY 2.____
   A. aid him to act in a depersonalized manner
   B. turn his interviewees into stereotyped affairs
   C. make the people he interviews feel manipulated
   D. give him a basis for critically examining his own practice

3. Compiling in advance a list of general questions to ask a client during an interview is a technique USUALLY considered 3.____
   A. *desirable*, chiefly because reference to the list will help keep the interview focused on the important issues
   B. *undesirable*, chiefly because use of such a list will discourage the client from speaking freely
   C. *desirable*, chiefly because the list will serve as a record of what questions were asked
   D. *undesirable*, chiefly because use of such a list will make the interview too mechanical and impersonal

4. The one of the following which is usually of GREATEST importance in winning the cooperation of a person being interviewed and while achieving the purpose of the interview is the interviewer's ability to 4.____
   A. gain the confidence of the person being interviewed
   B. stick to the subject of the interview
   C. handle a person who is obviously lying
   D. prevent the person being interviewed from withholding information

5. While interviewing clients, an interviewer should use the technique of interruption, beginning to speak when a client has temporarily paused at the end of a phrase or sentence, in order to 5.____
   A. limit the client's ability to voice his objections or complaints
   B. shorten, terminate or redirect a client's response
   C. assert authority when he feels that the client is too conceited
   D. demonstrate to the client that pauses in speech should be avoided

6. An interviewer might gain background information about a client by being aware of the person's speech during an interview. 6.____
   Which one of the following patterns of speech would offer the LEAST accurate information about a client? The

A. number of slang expressions and the level of vocabulary
B. presence and degree of an accent
C. rate of speech and the audibility level
D. presence of a physical speech defect

7. Suppose that you are interviewing a distressed client who claims that he was just laid off from his job and has no money to pay his rent. 7.____
Your FIRST action should be to
A. ask if he has sought other employment or has other sources of income
B. express your sympathy but explain that he must pay the rent on time
C. inquire about the reasons he was laid off from work
D. try to transfer him to a smaller apartment which he can afford

8. Suppose you have some background information on an applicant whom you are interviewing. During the interview, it appears that the applicant is giving you false information. 8.____
The BEST thing for you to do at that point is to
A. pretend that you are not aware of the written facts and let him continue
B. tell him what you already know and discuss the discrepancies with him
C. terminate the interview and make a note that the applicant is untrustworthy
D. tell him that, because he is making false statements, he will not be eligible for an apartment

9. A Spanish-speaking applicant may want to bring his bilingual child with him to an interview to act as an interpreter. 9.____
Which of the following would be LEAST likely to affect the value of an interview in which an applicant's child has act as interpreter?
A. It may make it undesirable to ask certain questions.
B. A child may do an inadequate job of interpretation.
C. A child's answers may indicate his feelings toward his parents.
D. The applicant may not want to reveal all information in front of his child.

10. Assume you are assigned to interview applicants. 10.____
Of the following, which is the BEST attitude for you to take in dealing with applicants?
A. Assume they will enjoy being interviewed because they believe that you have the power of decision
B. Expect that they have a history of anti-social behavior in the family, and probe deeply into the social development of family members
C. Expect that they will try to control the interview, thus you should keep them on the defensive
D. Assume that they will be polite and cooperative and attempt to secure the information you need in a business-like manner

11. If you are interviewing an applicant who is a minority group member in reference to his eligibility, it would be BEST for you to use language that is 11.____
A. *informal*, using ethnic expressions known to the applicant
B. *technical*, using the expressions commonly used in the agency

C. *simple*, using words and phrases which laymen understand
D. *formal* to remind the applicant that he is dealing with a government agency

12. When interviewing an applicant to determine his eligibility, it is MOST important to 12.____
A. have a prior mental picture of the typical eligible applicant
B. conduct the interview strictly according to a previously prepared script
C. keep in mind the goal of the interview, which is to determine eligibility
D. get an accurate and detailed account of the applicant's life history

13. The practice of trying to imagine yourself in the applicant's place during an interview is 13.____
A. *good*, mainly because you will be able to evaluate his responses better
B. *good*, mainly because it will enable you to treat him as a friend rather than as an applicant
C. *poor*, mainly because it is important for the applicant to see you as an impartial person
D. *poor*, mainly because it is too time-consuming to do this with each applicant

14. When dealing with clients from different ethnic backgrounds, you should be aware of certain tendencies toward prejudice. 14.____
Which of the following statements is LEAST likely to be valid?
A. Whites prejudiced against Blacks are more likely to be prejudiced against Hispanics than Whites not prejudiced against Blacks.
B. The less a White is in competition with Blacks, the less likely he is to be prejudiced against them.
C. Persons who have moved from one social group to another are likely to retain the attitudes and prejudices of their original social group.
D. When there are few Blacks or Hispanics in a project, Whites are less likely to be prejudiced against them than when there are many.

15. Of the following, the one who is MOST likely to be a good interviewer of people seeking assistance, is one who 15.____
A. tries to get applicants to apply to another agency instead
B. believes that it is necessary to get as much pertinent information as possible in order to determine the applicant's real needs
C. believes that people who seek assistance are likely to have persons with a history of irresponsible behavior in their households
D. is convinced that there is no need for a request for assistance

KEY (CORRECT ANSWERS)

1.	D	6.	C	11.	C
2.	D	7.	A	12.	C
3.	A	8.	B	13.	A
4.	A	9.	C	14.	C
5.	B	10.	D	15.	B

INTERVIEWING
EXAMINATION SECTION
TEST 1

DIRECTIONS: Each question or incomplete statement is followed by several suggested answers or completions. Select the one that BEST answers the question or completes the statement. *PRINT THE LETTER OF THE CORRECT ANSWER IN THE SPACE AT THE RIGHT.*

1. Of the methods given below for obtaining desired information from applicants, the one considered the BEST interviewing method is to 1.____
   A. work from an outline, asking the questions in the order in which they appear and requiring the applicant to give specific answers
   B. let the applicant tell what he has to say in his own way first, the interviewer then taking responsibility for asking questions on points not covered
   C. tell the applicant all the facts that it is necessary to have, then letting him give the information in any way he chooses
   D. verify all such facts as birth date, income, and past employment before seeing the applicant, then asking the applicant to fill in the remaining gaps when he is interviewed

2. Suppose an applicant objects to answering a question regarding his recent employment and asks, "What business is it of yours, young man?" 2.____
   In conducting the interview, the MOST constructive course of action for you to take under the circumstances would be to
   A. tell the applicant you have no intention of prying into his personal affairs and go on to the next question
   B. refer the applicant to your supervisor
   C. rephrase the question so that only a "Yes" or "No" answer is required
   D. explain why the question is being asked

3. An interview is BEST conducted in private PRIMARILY because 3.____
   A. the person interviewed will tend to be less self-conscious
   B. the interviewer will be able to maintain his continuity of thought better
   C. it will insure that the interview is "off the record"
   D. people tend to "show off" before an audience

4. An interviewer will be better able to understand the person interviewed and his problems if he recognizes that much of the person's behavior is due to motives 4.____
   A. which are deliberate
   B. of which he is unaware
   C. which are inexplicable
   D. which are kept under control

5. When an applicant is repeatedly told that "everything will be all right," the effect that can USUALLY be expected is that he will 5.____
   A. develop overt negativistic reactions toward the agency
   B. become too closely identified with the interviewer
   C. doubt the interviewer's ability to understand and help with his problems
   D. have greater confidence in the interviewer

6. While interviewing a client, it is PREFERABLE that the interviewer 6.____
   A. take no notes in order to avoid disturbing the client
   B. focus primary attention on the client while the client is talking
   C. take no notes in order to impress upon the client the interviewer's ability to remember all the pertinent facts of his case
   D. record all the details in order to show the client that what he says is important

7. During an interview, a curious applicant asks several questions about the interviewer's private life. 7.____
   As the interviewer, you should
   A. refuse to answer such questions
   B. answer his questions fully
   C. explain that your primary concern is with his problems and that discussion of your personal affairs will not be helpful in meeting his needs
   D. explain that it is the responsibility of the interviewer to ask questions and not to answer them

8. An interviewer can BEST establish a good relationship with the person being interviewed by 8.____
   A. assuming casual interest in the statements made by the person being interviewed
   B. asking questions which enable the person to show pride in his knowledge
   C. taking the point of view of the person interviewed
   D. showing a genuine interest in the person

9. An interviewer's attention must be directed toward himself as well as toward the person interviewed. 9.____
   This statement means that the interviewer should
   A. keep in mind the extent to which his own prejudices may influence his judgment
   B. rationalize the statements made by the person interviewed
   C. gain the respect and confidence of the person interviewed
   D. avoid being too impersonal

10. More complete expression will be obtained from a person being interviewed if the interviewer can create the impression that 10.____
   A. the data secured will become part of a permanent record
   B. official information must be accurate in every detail
   C. it is the duty of the person interviewed to give accurate data
   D. the person interviewed is participating in a discussion of his own problems

11. The practice of asking leading questions should be avoided in an interview because the 11.____
    A. interviewer risks revealing his attitudes to the person being interviewed
    B. interviewer may be led to ignore the objective attitudes of the person interviewed
    C. answers may be unwarrantedly influenced
    D. person interviewed will resent the attempt to lead him and will be less cooperative

12. A good technique for the interviewer to use in an effort to secure reliable data and to reduce the possibility of misunderstanding is to 12.____
    A. use casual undirected conversation, enabling the person being interviewed to talk about himself, and thus secure the desired information
    B. adopt the procedure of using direct questions regularly
    C. extract the desired information from the person being interviewed by putting him on the defensive
    D. explain to the person being interviewed the information desired and the reason for needing it

13. In interviewing an applicant, your attitude toward his veracity should be that the information he has furnished you is 13.____
    A. *untruthful* until you have had an opportunity to check the information
    B. *truthful* only insofar as verifiable facts are concerned
    C. *untruthful* because clients tend to interpret everything in their own favor
    D. *truthful* until you have information to the contrary

14. When an agency assigns its most experienced interviewers to conduct initial interviews with applicants, the MOST important reason for its action is that 14.____
    A. experienced workers are always older and, therefore, command the respect of applicants
    B. the applicant may be given a complete understanding of the procedures to be followed and the time involved in obtaining assistance
    C. applicants with fraudulent intentions will be detected, and prevented from obtaining further services from the agency
    D. the applicant may be given an understanding of the purpose of the assistance program and of the bases for granting assistance, in addition to the routine information

15. In conducting the first interview with an applicant, you should 15.____
    A. ask questions requiring "Yes" or "No" answers in order to simplify the interview
    B. rephrase several of the key questions as a check on his previous statements
    C. let him tell his own story while keeping him to the relevant facts
    D. avoid showing any sympathy for the applicant while he is revealing his personal needs and problems

16. When an interview opens an interview by asking the client direct questions about his work, it is very likely that the client will feel 16.____
   A. that the interview is interested in him
   B. at ease if his work has been good
   C. free to discuss his attitudes toward his work
   D. that good reports are of great importance to the interviewer in his thinking

17. When an interviewer does NOT understand the meaning of a response that a client has made, the interviewer should 17.____
   A. proceed to another topic
   B. state that he does not understand and ask for clarification
   C. act as if he understands so that the client's confidence in him should not be shaken
   D. ask the client to rephrase his response

18. When an interviewer makes a response which brings on a high degree of resistance in the client, he should 18.____
   A. apologize and rephrase his remark in a less evocative manner
   B. accept the resistance on the part of the client
   C. ignore the client's resistance
   D. recognize that little more will be accomplished in the interview and suggest another appointment

19. Most definitions of interviewing would NOT include the following as a necessary aspect: 19.____
   A. The interviewer and client meet face-to-face and talk things out
   B. The client is experiencing considerable emotional disturbance
   C. A valuable learning opportunity is provided for the client
   D. The interviewer brings a special competence to the relationship

20. A powerful dynamic in the interviewing process and often the very *antonym* of its counterpart in the instructional process is 20.____
   A. encouraging accuracy
   B. emphasizing structure
   C. pointing up sequential and orderly thinking
   D. processing ambiguity and equivocation

21. Interviewing techniques are frequently useful in working with clients. A basic fundamental is an atmosphere which may BEST be described as 21.____
   A. non-threatening
   B. motivating for creativity
   C. highly charged to stimulate excitement
   D. fairly-well structured

22. In interviewing the disadvantaged client, the subtle technique of steering away from high-level educational and vocational plans must be *replaced* by 22.____
   A. a wait-and-see explanation to the client
   B. the use of prediction tables to determine possibilities and probabilities of overcoming this condition

C. avoidance in discussing controversial issues of deprivation
D. encouragement and concrete consideration for planning his future

23. The process of collecting, analyzing, synthesizing, and interpreting information about the client should be 23.____
A. completed prior to interviewing
B. completed early in the interviewing process
C. limited to a type of interviewing which is primarily diagnostic in purpose
D. continuously pursued throughout interviewing

24. Catharsis, the "emotional unloading" of the client's feelings, has a value in the early stages of interviewing because it accomplishes all BUT which one of the following goals? 24.____
It
A. relieves strong physiological tensions in the client
B. increases the client's anxiety and aggrandizes his motivation to continue counseling
C. provides a strong substitute for "acting out" the client's feelings
D. releases emotional energy which the client has been using to bulwark his defenses

25. In the interviewing process, the interviewer should *usually* give information 25.____
A. whenever it is needed
B. at the end of the process
C. in the introductory interview
D. just before the client would ordinarily request it

KEY (CORRECT ANSWERS)

1. B
2. D
3. A
4. B
5. C

6. B
7. C
8. D
9. A
10. D

11. C
12. D
13. D
14. D
15. C

16. D
17. B
18. B
19. B
20. D

21. A
22. D
23. D
24. B
25. A

TEST 2

DIRECTIONS: Each question or incomplete statement is followed by several suggested answers or completions. Select the one that BEST answers the question or completes the statement. *PRINT THE LETTER OF THE CORRECT ANSWER IN THE SPACE AT THE RIGHT.*

1. Of the following problems that might affect the conduct and outcome of an interview, the MOST troublesome and usually the MOST difficult for the interviewer to control is the 1.____
   A. tendency of the interviewee to anticipate the needs and preferences of the interviewer
   B. impulse to cut the interviewee off when he seems to have reached the end of an idea
   C. tendency of interviewee attitude to bias the results
   D. tendency of the interviewer to do most of the talking

2. The supervisor MOST likely to be a good interviewer is one who 2.____
   A. is adept at manipulating people and circumstances toward his objective
   B. is able to put himself in the position of the interviewee
   C. gets the more difficult questions out of the way at the beginning of the interview
   D. develops one style and technique that can be used in any type of interview

3. A good interviewer guards against the tendency to form an overall opinion about an interviewee on the basis of a single aspect of the interviewee's makeup. 3.____
   This statement refers to a well-known source of error in interviewing known as the
   A. assumption error
   B. expectancy error
   C. extension effect
   D. halo effect

4. In conducting an "exit interview" with an employee who is leaving voluntarily, the interview's MAIN objective should be to 4.____
   A. see that the employee leaves with a good opinion of the organization
   B. learn the true reasons for the employee's resignation
   C. find out if the employee would consider a transfer
   D. try to get the employee to remain on the job

5. During an interview, an interviewee unexpectedly discloses a relevant but embarrassing personal fact. 5.____
   It would be BEST for the interviewer to
   A. listen calmly, avoiding any gesture or facial expression that would suggest approval or disapproval of what is related
   B. change the subject, since further discussion in this area may reveal other embarrassing, but irrelevant, personal facts

C. apologize to the interviewee for having led him to reveal such a fact and promise not to do so again
D. bring the interview to a close as quickly as possible in order to avoid a discussion which may be distressing to the interviewee

6. Suppose that, while you are interviewing an applicant for a position in your office, you notice a contradiction in facts in two of his responses. 6.____
For you to call the contradictions to his attention would be
A. *inadvisable*, because it reduces the interviewee's level of participation
B. *advisable*, because getting the facts is essential to a successful interview
C. *inadvisable*, because the interviewer should use more subtle techniques to resolve any discrepancies
D. *advisable*, because the interviewee should be impressed with the necessity for giving consistent answers

7. An interviewer should be aware that an undesirable result of including "leading questions" in an interview is to 7.____
A. cause the interviewee to give a "yes" or "no" answers with qualification or explanation
B. encourage the interviewee to discuss irrelevant topics
C. encourage the interviewee to give more meaningful information
D. reduce the validity of the information obtained from the interviewee

8. The kind of interview which is particularly helpful in getting an employee to tell about his complaints and grievances is one in which 8.____
A. a pattern has been worked out involving a sequence of exact questions to be asked
B. the interviewee is expected to support his statements with specific evidence
C. the interviewee is not made to answer specific questions but is encouraged to talk freely
D. the interviewer has specific items on which he wishes to get or give information

9. Suppose you are scheduled to interview an employee under your supervision concerning a health problem. You know that some of the questions you will be asking him will seem embarrassing to him, and that he may resist answering these questions. 9.____
In general, to hold these questions for the last part of the interview would be
A. *desirable*; the intervening time period gives the interviewer an opportunity to plan how to ask these sensitive questions.
B. *undesirable*; the employee will probably feel that he has been tricked when he suddenly must answer embarrassing questions
C. *desirable*; the employee will probably have increased confidence in the interviewer and be more willing to answer these questions
D. *undesirable*; questions that are important should not be deferred until the end of the interview

10. In conducting an interview, the BEST types of questions with which to begin the interview are those which the person interviewed is 10.____
 A. willing and able to answer
 B. willing but unable to answer
 C. able but unwilling to answer
 D. unable and unwilling to answer

11. In order to determine accurately a child's age, it is BEST for an interviewer to rely on 11.____
 A. the child's grade in school
 B. what the mother says
 C. birth records
 D. a library card

12. In his first interview with a new employee, it would be LEAST appropriate for a unit supervisor to 12.____
 A. find out the employee's preference for the several types of jobs to which he is able to assign him
 B. determine whether the employee will make good promotion material
 C. inform the employee of what his basic job responsibilities will be
 D. inquire about the employee's education and previous employment

13. If an interviewer takes care to phrase his questions carefully and precisely, the result will MOST probably be that 13.____
 A. he will be able to determine whether the person interviewed is being truthful
 B. the free flow of the interview will be lost
 C. he will get the information he wants
 D. he will ask stereotyped questions and narrow the scope of the interview

14. When, during an interview, is the person interviewed LEAST likely to be cautious about what he tells the interviewer? 14.____
 A. Shortly after the beginning when the questions normally suggest pleasant associations to the person interviewed
 B. As long as the interviewer keeps his questions to the point
 C. At the point where the person interviewed gains a clear insight into the area being discussed
 D. When the interview appears formally ended and goodbyes are being said

15. In an interview held for the purpose of getting information from the person interviewed, it is sometimes desirable for the interviewer to repeat the answer he has received to a question. 15.____
For the interviewer to rephrase such an answer in his own words is good practice MAINLY because it
 A. gives the interviewer time to make up his next question
 B. gives the person interviewed a chance to correct any possible misunderstanding
 C. gives the person interviewed the feeling that the interviewer considers his answer important
 D. prevents the person interviewed from changing his answer

16. There are several methods of formulating questions during an interview. The particular method used should be adapted to the interview problems presented by the person being questioned. 16.____
Of the following methods of formulating questions during an interview, the ACCEPTABLE one is for the interviewer to ask questions which
   A. incorporate several items in order to allow a cooperative interviewee freedom to organize his statements
   B. are ambiguous in order to foil a distrustful interviewee
   C. suggest the correct answer in order to assist an interviewee who appears confused
   D. would help an otherwise unresponsive interviewee to become more responsive

17. For an interviewer to permit the person being interviewed to read the data the interviewer writes as he records the person's responses on a routine departmental form is 17.____
   A. *desirable*, because it serves to assure the person interviewed that his responses are being recorded accurately
   B. *undesirable*, because it prevents the interviewer from clarifying uncertain points by asking additional questions
   C. *desirable*, because it makes the time that the person interviewed must wait while the answer is written seem shorter
   D. *undesirable*, because it destroys the confidentiality of the interview

18. Of the following methods of conducting an interview, the BEST is to 18.____
   A. ask questions with "yes" or "no" answers
   B. listen carefully and ask only questions that are pertinent
   C. fire questions at the interviewee so that he must answer sincerely and briefly
   D. read standardized questions to the person being interviewed

KEY (CORRECT ANSWERS)

1.	A	11.	C
2.	B	12.	B
3.	D	13.	C
4.	B	14.	D
5.	A	15.	B
6.	B	16.	D
7.	D	17.	A
8.	C	18.	B
9.	C		
10.	A		

EXAMINATION SECTION
TEST 1

DIRECTIONS: Each question or incomplete statement is followed by several suggested answers or completions. Select the one that BEST answers the question or completes the statement. *PRINT THE LETTER OF THE CORRECT ANSWER IN THE SPACE AT THE RIGHT.*

1. Deviant behavior is a sociological term used to describe behavior which is not in accord with generally accepted standards. This may include juvenile delinquency, adult criminality, mental or physical illness. 1.____
Comparison of normal with deviant behavior is useful to social workers because it

   A. makes it possible to establish watertight behavioral descriptions
   B. provides evidence of differential social behavior which distinguishes deviant from normal behavior
   C. indicates that deviant behavior is of no concern to social workers
   D. provides no evidence that social role is a determinant of behavior

2. Alcoholism may affect an individual client's ability to function as a spouse, parent, worker, and citizen. 2.____
A social worker's MAIN responsibility to a client with a history of alcoholism is to

   A. interpret to the client the causes of alcoholism as a disease syndrome
   B. work with the alcoholic's family to accept him as he is and stop trying to reform him
   C. encourage the family of the alcoholic to accept casework treatment
   D. determine the origins of his particular drinking problem, establish a diagnosis, and work out a treatment plan for him

3. There is a trend to regard narcotic addiction as a form of illness for which the current methods of intervention have not been effective. 3.____
Research on the combination of social, psychological, and physical causes of addiction would indicate that social workers should

   A. oppose hospitalization of addicts in institutions
   B. encourage the addict to live normally at home
   C. recognize that there is no successful treatment for addiction and act accordingly
   D. use the existing community facilities differentially for each addict

4. A study of social relationships among delinquent and non-delinquent youth has shown that 4.____

   A. delinquent youth generally conceal their true feelings and maintain furtive social contacts
   B. delinquents are more impulsive and vivacious than law-abiding boys
   C. non-delinquent youths diminish their active social relationships in order to sublimate any anti-social impulses
   D. delinquent and non-delinquent youths exhibit similar characteristics of impulsiveness and vivaciousness

5. The one of the following which is the CHIEF danger of interpreting the delinquent behavior of a child in terms of morality *alone* when attempting to get at its causes is that 5.____

   A. this tends to overlook the likelihood that the causes of the child's actions are more than a negation of morality and involve varied symptoms of disturbance
   B. a child's moral outlook toward life and society is largely colored by that of his parents, thus encouraging parent-child conflict
   C. too careful a consideration of the moral aspects of the offense and of the child's needs may often negate the demands of justice in a case
   D. standards of morality may be of no concern to the delinquent and he may not realize the seriousness of his offenses

6. Experts in the field of personnel administration are generally agreed that an employee should not be under the immediate supervision of more than one supervisor. A certain worker, because of an emergency situation, divides his time equally between two limited caseloads on a prearranged time schedule. Each unit has a different supervisor, and the worker performs substantially the same duties in each caseload. 6.____
   The above statement is pertinent in this situation CHIEFLY because

   A. each supervisor, feeling that the cases in her unit should have priority, may demand too much of the worker's time
   B. the two supervisors may have different standards of work performance and may prefer different methods of doing the work
   C. the worker works part-time on each caseload and may not have full knowledge or control of the situation in either caseload
   D. the task of evaluating the worker's services will be doubled, with two supervisors instead of one having to rate his work

7. Experts in modern personnel management generally agree that employees on all job levels should be permitted to offer suggestions for improving work methods. 7.____
   Of the following, the CHIEF limitation of such suggestions is that they may, at times,

   A. be offered primarily for financial reward and not show genuine interest in improvement of work methods
   B. be directed towards making individual jobs easier
   C. be restricted by the employees' fear of radically changing the work methods favored by their supervisors
   D. show little awareness of the effects on the overall objectives and functions of the entire agency

8. Through the supervisory process and relationship, the supervisor is trying to help workers gain increased self-awareness. 8.____
   Of the following statements concerning this process, the one which is MOST accurate is:

   A. Self-awareness is developed gradually so that worker can learn to control his own reactions.
   B. Worker is expected to be introspective primarily for his own enlightenment.
   C. Supervisor is trying to help worker handle any emotional difficulties he may reveal.
   D. Worker is expected at the onset to share and determine with the supervisor what in his previous background makes it difficult for him to use certain ideas.

9. The one of the following statements concerning principles in the learning process which is LEAST accurate is: 9.____

A. Some degree of regression on the part of the worker is usually natural in the process of development and this should be accepted by the supervisor.
B. When a beginning worker shows problems, the supervisor should first handle this behavior as a personality difficulty.
C. It has been found in the work training process that some degree of resistance is usually inevitable.
D. The emotional content of work practice may tend to set up *blind spots* in workers.

10. Of the following, the one that represents the BEST basis for planning the content of a successful staff development program is the 10.____

A. time available for meetings
B. chief social problems of the community
C. common needs of the staff workers as related to the situations with which they are dealing
D. experimental programs conducted by other agencies

11. In planning staff development seminars, the MOST valuable topics for discussion are likely to be those selected from 11.____

A. staff suggestions based on the staff's interest and needs
B. topics recommended for consideration by professional organizations
C. topics selected by the administration based on demonstrated limitations of staff skill and knowledge
D. topics selected by the administration based on a combination of staff interest and objectivity evaluated staff needs

12. Staff meetings designed to promote professional staff development are MOST likely to achieve this goal when 12.____

A. there is the widest participation among all staff members who attend the meetings
B. participation by the most skilled and experienced staff members is predominant
C. participation by selected staff members is planned before the meeting sessions
D. supervisory personnel take major responsibility for participation

13. Assume that you are the leader of a conference attended by representatives of various city and private agencies. After the conference has been underway for a considerable time, you realize that the representative of one of these agencies has said nothing.
It would generally be BEST for you to 13.____

A. ask him if he would like to say anything
B. ask the group a pertinent question that he would probably be best able to answer
C. make no special effort to include him in the conversation
D. address the next question you planned to ask to him directly

14. A member of a decision-making conference generally makes his BEST contribution to the conference when he 14.____

A. compromises on his own point of view and accepts most of the points of other conference members
B. persuades the conference to accept all or most of his points

C. persuades the conference to accept his major proposals but will yield on the minor ones
D. succeeds in integrating his ideas with the ideas of the other conference members

15. Of the following, the LEAST accurate statement concerning the compilation and use of statistics in administration is: 15.___

A. Interpretation of statistics is as necessary as their compilation.
B. Statistical records of expenditures and services are one of the bases for budget preparation.
C. Statistics on the quality of services rendered to the community will clearly delineate the human values achieved.
D. The results achieved from collecting and compiling statistics must be in keeping with the cost and effort required.

16. An important administrative problem is how precisely to define the limits on authority that is delegated to subordinate supervisors. 16.___
Such definition of limits of authority SHOULD be

A. as precise as possible and practicable in all areas
B. as precise as possible and practicable in all areas of function,but should allow considerable flexibility in the area of personnel management
C. as precise as possible and practicable in the area of personnel management, but should allow considerable flexibility in the areas of function
D. in general terms so as to allow considerable flexibility both in the areas of function and in the areas of personnel management

17. The LEAST important of the following reasons why a particular activity should be assigned to a unit which performs activities dissimilar to it is that 17.___

A. close coordination is needed between the particular activity and other activities performed by the unit
B. it will enhance the reputation and prestige of the unit supervisor
C. the unit makes frequent use of the results of this particular activity
D. the unit supervisor has a sound knowledge and understanding of the particular activity

18. The MOST important of the following reasons why the average resident of a deteriorated slum neighborhood resists relocation to an area in the suburbs with better physical accommodations is that he 18.___

A. does not recognize as undesirable the characteristics which are responsible for deterioration of the neighborhood
B. has some expectation of neighborly assistance in his old home in times of stress and adversity
C. hopes for better days when he may be able to become a figure of some importance and envy in the old neighborhood
D. is attuned to the noise of the city and fears the quiet of the suburb

19. From a psychological and sociological point of view, the MOST important of the following dangers to the persons living in an economically depressed area in which the only step taken by governmental and private social agencies to assist these persons is the granting of a dole is that 19.____

A. industry will be reluctant to expand its operations in that area
B. the dole will encourage additional non-producers to enter the area
C. the residents of the area will probably have to find their own solution to their problems
D. their permanent dependency will be fostered

20. The term *real wages* is GENERALLY used by economists to mean the 20.____

A. amount of take-home pay left after taxes, social security, and other such deductions have been made by the employer
B. average wage actually earned during a calendar or fiscal year
C. family income expressed on a per capita basis
D. wages expressed in terms of its buyer power

21. It has, at times, been suggested that an effective way to eradicate juvenile delinquency would be to arrest and punish the parents for the criminal actions of their delinquent children. 21.____
The one of the following which is the CHIEF defect of this proposal is that

A. it fails to get at the cause of the delinquent act and tends to further weaken disturbed parent-child relationships
B. since the criminally inclined child has apparently demonstrated little love or affection for his parent, the child will be unlikely to amend his behavior in order to avoid hurting his parent
C. the child who commits anti-social acts does so in many cases in order to hurt his parents so that this proposal would not only increase the parents' sorrow, but would also serve as an incentive to more delinquency by the child
D. the punishment should be limited to the person who commits the illegal action rather than to those who are most interested in his welfare

22. Surveys which have compared the relative stability of marriages between white persons with marriages between non-white persons in this country have shown that, among Blacks, there is 22.____

A. a significantly higher percentage of spouses absent from the household than among whites
B. a significantly higher percentage of spouses absent from the household than among whites living in the South, but the opposite is true in the Northeast
C. a significantly lower percentage of spouses absent from the household than among whites
D. no significant difference in the percentage of spouses absent from the household when compared with the white population

23. A phenomenon found in the cultural and recreational patterns of European immigrant families in America is that, generally, the foreign-born adults 23.____

A. as well as their children, tend soon to forget their old-world activities and adopt the cultural and recreational customs of America
B. as well as their children, tend to retain and continue their old-world cultural and recreational pursuits, and find it equally difficult to adopt those of America
C. tend soon to drop their old pursuits and adopt the cultural and recreational patterns of America while their children find it somewhat more difficult to make this change
D. tend to retain and continue their old-world cultural and recreational pursuits while their children tend to rapidly replace these by the games and cultural patterns of America

24. Certain mores of migrant groups are strengthened under the impact of their contact with the native society while other mores are weakened. 24.____
In the case of Puerto Ricans who have come to the city, the effect of such contact upon their traditional family structure has been a

A. strengthening of the former maternalistic family structure
B. strengthening of the former paternalistic family structure
C. weakening of the former maternalistic family structure
D. weakening of the former paternalistic family structure

25. Administrative reviews and special studies of independent experts, as reported by the Department of Health, Education and Welfare, indicate that the proportion of recipients of public assistance who receive such assistance through *wilful misrepresentation* of the facts is 25.____

A. less than 1%
B. about 4%
C. between 4% and 7%
D. between 7% and 10%

KEY (CORRECT ANSWERS)

1. B
2. D
3. D
4. B
5. A

6. B
7. D
8. A
9. B
10. C

11. D
12. A
13. B
14. D
15. C

16. A
17. B
18. B
19. D
20. D

21. A
22. A
23. D
24. D
25. A

TEST 2

DIRECTIONS: Each question or incomplete statement is followed by several suggested answers or completions. Select the one that BEST answers the question or completes the statement. *PRINT THE LETTER OF THE CORRECT ANSWER IN THE SPACE AT THE RIGHT.*

1. In order to meet more adequately the public assistance needs occasioned by sudden changes in the national economy, social service agencies, in general, recommend, as a matter of preference, that 1.____

   A. each locality build up reserve funds to care for needy unemployed persons in order to avoid a breakdown of local resources such as occurred during the depression
   B. the federal government assume total responsibility for the administration of public assistance
   C. state settlement laws be strictly enforced so that unemployed workers will be encouraged to move from the emergency industry centers to their former homes
   D. a federal-state-local program of general assistance be established with need as the only eligibility requirement
   E. eligibility requirements be tightened to assure that only legitimately worthy local residents receive the available assistance

2. The MOST practical method of maintaining income for the majority of aged persons who are no longer able to work, or for the families of those workers who are deceased, is a(n) 2.____

   A. comprehensive system of non-categorical assistance on a basis of cash payments
   B. integrated system of public assistance and extensive work relief programs
   C. co-ordinated system of providing care in institutions and foster homes
   D. system of contributory insurance in which a cash benefit is paid as a matter of right
   E. expanded system of diagnostic and treatment centers

3. With the establishment of insurance and assistance programs under the Social Security Act, many institutional programs for the aged have tended to the greatest extent toward an increased emphasis on providing, of the following types of assistance, 3.____

   A. care for the aged by denominational groups
   B. care for children requiring institutional treatment
   C. recreational facilities for the able-bodied aged
   D. training facilities in industrial homework for the aged
   E. care for the chronically ill and infirm aged

4. Of the following terms, the one which BEST describes the Social Security Act is 4.____

   A. enabling legislation
   B. regulatory statute
   C. appropriations act
   D. act of mandamus
   E. provisional enactment

5. Of the following, the term which MOST accurately describes an appropriation is 5.___

A. authority to spend
B. itemized estimate
C. *fund* accounting
D. anticipated expenditure
E. executive budget

6. When business expansion causes a demand for labor, the worker group which benefits MOST immediately is the group comprising 6.___

A. employed workers
B. inexperienced workers under 21 years of age
C. experienced workers 21 to 25 years of age
D. inexperienced older workers
E. experienced workers over 40 years of age

7. The MOST important failure in our present system of providing social work services in local communities is the 7.___

A. absence of adequate facilities for treating mental illness
B. lack of coordination of available data and service in the community
C. poor quality of the casework services provided by the public agencies
D. limitations of the probation and parole services
E. inadequacy of private family welfare services

8. Recent studies of the relationship between incidence of illness and the use of available treatment services among various population groups in the United States show that 8.___

A. while lower-income families use medical services with greater frequency, total expenditures are greater among the upper-income groups
B. although the average duration of a period of medical care increases with increasing income, the average frequency of obtaining care decreases with increasing income
C. adequacy of medical service is inversely related to frequency of illness and size of family income
D. families in the higher-income brackets have a heavier incidence of illness and make greater use of medical services than do those in the lower-income brackets
E. both as to frequency and duration, the distribution of illness falls equally on all groups, but the use of medical services increases with income

9. The category of disease which most public health departments and authorities usually are NOT equipped to handle *directly* is that of 9.___

A. chronic disease
B. bronchial disturbances
C. venereal disease
D. mosquito-borne diseases
E. incipient forms of tuberculosis

10. Recent statistical analyses of the causes of death in the United States indicate that medical science has now reached the stage where it would be preferable to increase its research toward control, among the following, PRINCIPALLY of 10.____

A. accidents
B. suicides
C. communicable disease
D. chronic disease
E. infant mortality

11. Although the distinction between mental disease and mental deficiency is fairly definite, both these conditions USUALLY represent 11.____

A. diseases of one part or organ of the body rather than of the whole person
B. an inadequacy existing from birth or shortly afterwards and appearing as a simplicity of intelligence
C. a deficiency developing later in life and characterized by distortions of attitude and belief
D. inadequacies in meeting life situations and in conducting one's affairs
E. somewhat transitory conditions characterized by disturbances of consciousness

12. According to studies made by reliable medical research organizations in the United States, differences among the states in proportion of physicians to population are MOST directly related to the 12.____

A. geographic resources among the states
B. skill of the physicians
C. relative proportions of urban and rural people in the population of the states
D. number of specialists in the ranks of the physicians
E. health status of the people in the various states

13. One of the MAIN advantages of incorporating a charitable organization is that 13.____

A. gifts or property of a corporation cannot be held in perpetuity
B. gifts to unincorporated charitable organizations are not deductible from the taxable income
C. incorporation gives less legal standing or *personality* than an informal partnership
D. members of a corporation cannot be held liable for debts contracted by the organization
E. a corporate organization cannot be sued

14. The BASIC principle underlying a social security program is that the government should provide 14.____

A. aid to families that is not dependent on state or local participation
B. assistance to any worthy family unable to maintain itself independently
C. protection to individuals against some of the social risks that are inherent in an industrialized society
D. safeguards against those factors leading to economic depression

15. The activities of state and local public welfare agencies are dependent to a large degree on the public assistance program of the federal government. 15.___
The one of the following which the federal government has NOT been successful in achieving within the local agencies is the

A. broadening of the scope of public assistance administration
B. expansion of the categorical programs
C. improvement of the quality of service given to clients
D. standardization of the administration of general assistance programs

16. Of the following statements, the one which BEST describes the federal government's position, as stated in the Social Security Act, with regard to tests of character or fitness to be administered by local or state welfare departments to prospective clients is that 16.___

A. no tests of character are required but they are not specifically prohibited
B. if tests of character are used, they must be uniform throughout the state
C. tests of character are contrary to the philosophy of the federal government and are to be considered illegal
D. no tests of character are required, and assistance to those states that use them will be withheld

17. An increase in the size of the welfare grant may increase the cost of the welfare program not only in terms of those already on the welfare rolls, but because it may result in an increase in the number of people on the rolls. 17.___
The CHIEF reason that an increase in the size of the grant may cause an increase in the number of people on the rolls is that the increased grant may

A. induce low-salaried wage earners to apply for assistance rather than continue at their menial jobs
B. make eligible for assistance many people whose resources are just above the previous standard
C. induce many people to apply for assistance who hesitated to do so because of meagerness of the previous grant
D. make relatives less willing to contribute because the welfare grant can more adequately cover their dependents' needs

18. One of the MAIN differences between the use of casework methods by a public welfare agency and by a private welfare agency is that the public welfare agency 18.___

A. requires that the applicant be eligible for the services it offers
B. cannot maintain a non-judgmental attitude toward its clients because of legal requirements
C. places less emphasis on efforts to change the behavior of its clients
D. must be more objective in its approach to the client because public funds are involved

19. All definitions of social casework include certain major assumptions. 19.___
Of the following, the one which is NOT considered a major assumption is that

A. the individual and society are interdependent
B. social forces influence behavior and attitudes, affording opportunity for self-development and contribution to the world in which we live
C. reconstruction of the total personality and reorganization of the total environment are specific goals
D. the client is a responsible participant at every step in the solution of his problems

20. In order to provide those services to problem families which will help restore them to a self-maintaining status, it is necessary to FIRST 20.____

A. develop specific plans to meet the individual needs of the problem family
B. reduce the size of those caseloads composed of multi-problem families
C. remove them from their environment and provide them with the means of overcoming their dependency
D. identify the factors causing their dependency and creating problems for them

21. Of the following, the type of service which can provide the client with the MOST enduring help is that service which 21.____

A. provides him with material aid and relieves the stress of his personal problems
B. assists him to do as much as he can for himself and leaves him free to make his own decisions
C. directs his efforts towards returning to a self-maintaining status and provides him with desirable goals
D. gives him the feeling that the agency is interested in him as an individual and stands ready to assist him with his problems

22. Psychiatric interpretation of unconscious motivations can bring childhood conflicts into the framework of adult understanding and open the way for them to be resolved, but the interpretation must come from within the client. 22.____
This statement means MOST NEARLY that

A. treatment is merely diagnosis in reverse
B. explaining a client to himself will lead to the resolution of his problems
C. the client must arrive at an understanding of his problems
D. unresolved childhood conflicts create problems for the adult

23. A significant factor in the United States economic picture is the state of the labor market. 23.____
Of the following, the MOST important development affecting the labor market has been

A. an expansion of the national defense effort creating new plant capacity
B. the general increase in personal income as a result of an increase in overtime pay in manufacturing industries
C. the growth of manufacturing as a result of automation
D. a demand for a large number of jobs resulting from new job applicants as well as from displacement of workers by automation

24. A typical characteristic of the United States population over 65 is that MOST of them 24.____

A. are independent and capable of self-support
B. live in their own homes but require various supportive services
C. live in institutions for the aged
D. require constant medical attention at home or in an institution

25. The one of the following factors which is MOST important in preventing persons 65 years of age and older from getting employment is the 25.____

A. misconceptions by employers of skills and abilities of senior citizens
B. lack of skill in modern industrial techniques of persons in this age group
C. social security laws restricting employment of persons in this age group
D. unwillingness of persons in this age group to continue supporting themselves

KEY (CORRECT ANSWERS)

1. D
2. D
3. E
4. A
5. A
6. B
7. B
8. C
9. A
10. D
11. D
12. C
13. D
14. C
15. D
16. A
17. B
18. C
19. C
20. D
21. B
22. C
23. D
24. B
25. A

EXAMINATION SECTION

TEST 1

DIRECTIONS: Each question or incomplete statement is followed by several suggested answers or completions. Select the one that BEST answers the question or completes the statement. *PRINT THE LETTER OF THE CORRECT ANSWER IN THE SPACE AT THE RIGHT.*

1. When a worker is planning a future interview with a client, of the following, the MOST important consideration is the 1.____
   A. recommendations he will make to the client
   B. place where the client will be interviewed
   C. purpose for which the client will be interviewed
   D. personality of the client

2. For a worker to make a practice of reviewing the client's case record, if available, prior to the interview is usually 2.____
   A. *inadvisable*, because knowledge of the client's past record will tend to influence the worker's judgment
   B. *advisable*, because knowledge of the client's background will help the worker to identify discrepancies in the client's responses
   C. *inadvisable*, because such review is time-consuming and of questionable value
   D. *advisable*, because knowledge of the client's background will help the worker to understand the client's situation

3. Assume that a worker makes a practice of constantly re-assuring clients with serious and complex problems by making such statements as: *I'm sure you'll soon be well; I know you'll get a job soon*; or *Everything will be all right.* 3.____
   Of the following, the MOST likely result of such practice is to
   A. encourage the client and make him feel that the worker understands what the client is going through
   B. make the client doubtful about the worker's understanding of his difficulties and the worker's ability to help
   C. confuse the client and cause him to hesitate to take any action on his own initiative
   D. help the client to be more realistic about his situation and the probability that it will improve

4. In order to get the maximum amount of information from a client during an interview, of the following, it is MOST important for the worker to communicate to the client the feeling that the worker is 4.____
   A. interested in the client
   B. a figure of authority
   C. efficient in his work habits
   D. sympathetic to the client's lifestyle

5. Of the following, the worker who takes extremely detailed notes during an interview with a client is MOST likely to 5.____
   A. encourage the client to talk freely
   B. distract and antagonize the client
   C. help the client feel at ease
   D. understand the client's feelings

6. You find that many of the clients you interview are verbally abusive and unusually hostile to you. 6.____
   Of the following, the MOST appropriate action for you to take FIRST is to
   A. review your interviewing techniques and consider whether you may be provoking these clients
   B. act in a more authoritative manner when interviewing troublesome clients
   C. tell these clients that you will not process their applications unless their troublesome behavior ceases
   D. disregard the clients' troublesome behavior during the interviews

7. During an interview, you did not completely understand several of your client's responses. In each instance, you rephrased the client's statement and asked the client if that was what he meant. 7.____
   For you to use such a technique during interviews would be considered
   A. *inappropriate*; you may have distorted the client's meaning by rephrasing his statements
   B. *inappropriate*; you should have asked the same question until you received a comprehensible response
   C. *appropriate*; the client will have a chance to correct you if you have misinterpreted his responses
   D. *appropriate*; a worker should rephrase clients' responses for the records

8. A worker is interviewing a client who has just had a severe emotional shock because of an assault on her by a mugger. 8.____
   Of the following, the approach which would generally be MOST helpful to the client is for the worker to
   A. comfort the client and encourage her to talk about the assault
   B. sympathize with the client but refuse to talk about the assault
   C. tell the client to control her emotions and think positively about the future
   D. proceed with the interview in an impersonal and unemotional manner

9. A worker finds that her questions are misinterpreted by many of the clients she interviews. 9.___
   Of the following, the MOST likely reason for this problem is that the
   A. client is not listening attentively
   B. client wants to avoid the subject being discussed
   C. worker has failed to express her meaning clearly
   D. worker has failed to put the client at ease

10. For a worker to look directly at the client and observe him during the interview is, generally, 10.____
   A. *inadvisable*; this will make the client nervous and uncomfortable
   B. *advisable*; the client will be more likely to refrain from lying
   C. *inadvisable*; the worker will not be able to take notes for the case record
   D. *advisable*; this will encourage conversation and accelerate the progress of the interview

11. You are interviewing a client who is applying for social services for the first time. In order to encourage this client to freely give you the information needed for you to establish his eligibility, of the following, the BEST way to start the interview is by 11.____
   A. asking questions the client can easily answer
   B. conveying the impression that his responses to your questions will be checked
   C. asking two or three similar but important questions
   D. assuring the client that your sole responsibility is *getting the facts*

12. Workers are encouraged to record significant information obtained from clients and services provided for clients. 12.____
Of the following, the MOST important reason for this practice is that these case records will
   A. help to reduce the need for regular supervisory conferences
   B. indicate to workers which clients are taking up the most time
   C. provide information which will help the agency to improve its services to clients
   D. make it easier to verify the complaints of clients

13. As a worker in the employment eligibility section, you find that interviews can be completed in a shorter period of time if you ask questions which limit the client to a certain answer. 13.____
For you to use such a technique would be considered
   A. *inappropriate*, because this type of question usually requires advance preparation
   B. *inappropriate*, because this type of question may inhibit the client from saying what he really means
   C. *appropriate*, because you know the areas into which the questions should be directed
   D. *appropriate*, because this type of question usually helps clients to express themselves clearly

14. Assume that a worker at a juvenile detention center is planning foster care placement for a child. 14.____
For the worker to have the child participate in the planning is generally considered to be
   A. time-consuming and of little practical value in preparing the child for placement
   B. valuable in helping the child adjust to future placement

C. useful, because the child will be more likely to cooperate with others in the center
D. anxiety-provoking because the child will feel that he has been abandoned

15. You have been assigned to interview the mother of a five-year-old son in her home to get information useful in locating the child's absent father. During the interview, you notice many serious bruises on the child's arms and legs, which the mother explains are due to the child's clumsiness. 15.____
Of the following, your BEST course of action is to
A. accept the mother's explanation and concentrate on getting information which will help you to locate the father
B. advise the mother to have the child examined for a medical condition that may be causing his clumsiness
C. make a surprise visit to the mother later, to see whether someone is beating the child
D. complete your interview with the mother and report the case to your supervisor for investigation of possible child abuse

16. During an interview, the former landlord of an absent father offers to help you to locate the father if you will give the landlord confidential information you have on the financial situation of the father. 16.____
Of the following, you should
A. immediately end the interview with the landlord
B. urge the landlord to help you but explain that you are not permitted to give him confidential information
C. freely give the landlord the confidential information he requests about the father
D. give the landlord the information only if he promises to keep it confidential

17. You feel that your client, a released mental patient, is not adjusting well to living on his own in an apartment. To gather more information, you interview privately his next-door neighbor, who claims that the client is creating a disturbance and speaks of the client in an angry and insulting manner. 17.____
Of the following, the BEST action for you to take in this situation is to
A. listen patiently to the neighbor to try to get the facts about your client's behavior
B. inform the neighbor that he has no right to speak insultingly about a mentally ill person
C. make an appointment to interview the neighbor some other time when he isn't so upset
D. tell the neighbor that you were not aware of the client's behavior and that you will have the client moved

18. As a worker assigned to an income maintenance center, you are interviewing a client to determine his eligibility for a work program. Suddenly, the client begins to shout that he is in no condition to work and that you are persecuting him for no reason. 18.____

Of the following, your BEST response to this client is to
A. advise the client to stop shouting or you will call for the security guard
B. wait until the client calms down, then order him to come back for another interview
C. insist that you are not persecuting the client and that he must complete the interview
D. wait until the client calms down, say that you understand how he feels, and try to continue the interview

19. You are counseling a mother whose 17-year-old son has recently been returned home from a mental institution. Although she is willing to care for her son at home, she is frightened by his strange and sometimes violent behavior and does not know the best arrangement to make for his care. 19.____
Of the following, your MOST appropriate response to this mother's problem is to
A. describe the supportive services and alternatives to home care which are available
B. help her to accept her son's strange and violent behavior
C. tell her that she will not be permitted to care for her son at home if she is frightened by his behavior
D. convince her that she is not responsible for her son's mental condition

20. Assume that, as an intake worker, you are interviewing an elderly man who comes to the center several times a month to discuss topics with you which are not related to social service. You realize that the man is lonely and enjoys these conversations. 20.____
Of the following, it would be MOST appropriate to
A. politely discourage the man from coming in to pass the time with you
B. avoid speaking to this man the next time he comes into the center
C. explore with the client his feelings about joining a Senior Citizens' Center
D. continue to hold these conversations with the man

21. A client you are interviewing in the housing elibility section tends to ramble on after each response that he gives, so that man clients are kept waiting. 21.____
In this situation, of the following, it would be MOST advisable to
A. try to direct the interview, in order to obtain the necessary information
B. reduce the number of questions asked so that you can shorten the interview
C. arrange a second interview for the client so that you can give him more time
D. tell the client that he is wasting everybody's time

22. A non-minority worker in an employment eligibility unit is about to interview a minority client on public assistance for job placement when the client says: *What does your kind know about my problems? You've never had to survive out on these streets.* 22.____
Of the following, the worker's MOST appropriate response to this situation is to

A. postpone the interview until a minority worker is available to interview the client
B. tell the client that he must cooperate with the worker if he wants to continue receiving public assistance
C. explain to the client the function of the worker in this unit and the services he provides
D. assure the client that you do not have to be a member of a minority group to understand the effects of poverty

23. As a worker in a family services unit, you have been assigned to follow-up a case folder recently forwarded from the protective-diagnostic unit. 23.____
After making appropriate clerical notations in your records such as name of client and date of receipt, which of the following would be the MOST appropriate step to take next?
A. Confer with your supervisor
B. Read and review all reports included in the case folder
C. Arrange to visit with the client at his home
D. Confer with representatives of any other agencies which have been in contact with the client

24. As a worker in the employment section, you are interviewing a young client who seriously underestimates the amount of education and training he will require for a certain occupation. 25.____
For you to tell the client that you think he is mistaken would, generally, be considered
A. *inadvisable*, because workers should not express their opinions to clients
B. *inadvisable*, because clients have the right to self-determination
C. *advisable*, because clients should generally be alerted to their misconceptions
D. *advisable*, because workers should convince clients to adopt a proper lifestyle

25. As an intake worker, you are counseling a mother and her unmarried, thirteen-year-old daughter, who is six months pregnant, concerning the advisability of placing the daughter's baby for adoption. The mother insists on adoption, but the daughter remains silent and appears undecided. 25.____
Of the following, you should encourage the daughter to
A. make the final decision on adoption herself
B. keep her baby despite her mother's insistence on adoption
C. accept her mother's insistence on adoption
D. make the decision on adoption together with her mother

KEY (CORRECT ANSWERS)

1. C
2. D
3. B
4. A
5. B

6. A
7. C
8. A
9. C
10. D

11. A
12. C
13. B
14. B
15. D

16. B
17. A
18. D
19. A
20. C

21. A
22. C
23. B
24. C
25. D

TEST 2

DIRECTIONS: Each question or incomplete statement is followed by several suggested answers or completions. Select the one that BEST answers the question or completes the statement. *PRINT THE LETTER OF THE CORRECT ANSWER IN THE SPACE AT THE RIGHT.*

1. You are interviewing a legally responsible absent father who refuses to make child support payments because he claims the mother physically abuses the child. 1.____
Of the following, the BEST way for you to handle his situation is to tell the father that you
   A. will report his complaint about the mother, but he is still responsible for making child support payments
   B. suspect that he is complaining about the mother in order to avoid his own responsibility for making child support payments
   C. are concerned with his responsibility to make child support payments, not with the mother's abuse of the child
   D. cannot determine his responsibility for making child support payments until his complaint about the mother is investigated

2. On a visit to a home where child abuse is alleged, you find the mother preparing lunch for her two children. She tells you that she knows that a neighbor is spreading lies about her treatment of the children. 2.____
Which one of the following is the BEST action for you to take?
   A. Thank the mother for her assistance, leave the home, and indicate in your report that the allegation of child abuse is false
   B. Tell the mother that, since you have been sent to visit her, there must be some truth to the allegations
   C. Explain the purpose of your visit and observe whatever interaction takes place between the children and the mother
   D. Conclude the interview, since you have observed the mother preparing a good lunch for the children

3. You are interviewing an elderly woman who lives alone to determine her eligibility for homemaker service at public expense. Though obviously frail and in need of this service, the woman is not completely cooperative, and, during the interview, is often silent for a considerable period of time. 3.____
Of the following, the BEST way for you to deal with these periods of silence is to
   A. realize that she may be embarrassed to have to apply for homemaker service at public expense, and emphasize her right to this service
   B. postpone the interview and make an appointment with her for a later date, when she may be better able to cooperate
   C. explain to the woman that you have many clients to interview and need her cooperation to complete the interview quickly
   D. recognize that she is probably hiding something and begin to ask questions to draw her out

4. During a conference with an adolescent boy at a juvenile detention center, you find out for the first time that he would prefer to be placed in foster care rather than return to his natural parents. 1.____
To uncover the reasons why the boy dislikes his own home, of the following, it would be MOST advisable for you to
   A. ask the boy a number of short, simple questions about his feelings
   B. encourage the boy to talk freely and express his feelings as best he can
   C. interview the parents and find out why the boy doesn't want to live at home
   D. administer a battery of psychological tests in order to make an assessment of the boy's problems

5. Of the following, the BEST way to determine which activities should be provided for members of a Senior Citizens' Center is to 5.____
   A. ask the neighborhood community board to submit their recommendations
   B. meet with the professional staff of the center to get their opinions
   C. encourage the members of the center to express their personal preferences
   D. study the schedules prepared by other Senior Citizens' Centers for guidance

6. You are interviewing a mother who is applying for Aid to Families with Dependent Children because the husband has deserted the family. The mother becomes annoyed at having to answer your questions and tells you to leave her apartment. 6.____
Which one of the following actions would be MOST appropriate to take FIRST in this situation?
   A. Return to the office and close the case for lack of cooperation
   B. Tell the mother that you will get the information from her neighbors if she does not cooperate
   C. Tell the mother that you must stay until you get answers to your questions
   D. Explain to the mother the reasons for the interview and the consequences of her failure to cooperate

7. A worker assigned to visit homebound clients to determine their eligibility for Medicaid must understand each client's situation as completely as possible. 7.____
Of the following source which may provide insight into the client's situation, the one that is generally MOST revealing is:
   A. Close relatives of the client, who have known him for many years
   B. Next-door neighbors, who have observed the daily living habits of the client
   C. The client himself, who can provide his own description of his situation
   D. The records of other social agencies that may have served the client

8. A worker counseling juvenile clients finds that, although he can tolerate most of their behavior, he becomes infuriated when they lie to him. 8.____
Of the following, the worker can BEST deal with his anger at his clients' lying by

A. recognizing his feelings of anger and learning to control expression of these feelings to his clients
B. warning his clients that he cannot be responsible for his anger when a client lies to him
C. using willpower to suppress his feelings of anger when a client lies to him
D. realizing that lying is a common trait of juveniles and not directed against him personally

9. During an interview at the employment eligibility section, one of your clients, a former drug addict, has expressed an interest in attending a community counseling center and resuming his education. 9.____
In this case, the MOST appropriate action that you should take FIRST is to
A. determine whether this ambition is realistic for a former drug addict
B. send the client's application to a community counseling center which provides services to former addicts
C. ask the client whether he is really motivated or is just seeking your approval
D. encourage and assist the client to take this step, since his interest is a positive sign

10. Because of habitual neglect by his mother, a five-year-old boy has been placed in a foster home. 10.____
For the worker to encourage the mother to visit the boy in the foster home is, generally,
A. *desirable*, because the boy will be helped by continuing his ties with his mother
B. *undesirable*, because the boy will be upset by his mother's visits and will have a harder time adjusting to the foster home
C. *desirable*, because the mother will learn from the foster parents how she should treat the boy
D. *undesirable*, because the mother should be punished for her neglect of the boy by complete separation from him

11. You are interviewing a client who, during previous appointments, has not responded to your requests for information required to determine his continued eligibility for services. On this occasion, the client again offers an excuse which you feel is not acceptable. 11.____
For you to advise the client of the probable loss of services because of his lack of cooperation is
A. *inappropriate*, because the threat to withhold services will harm the relationship between worker and client
B. *inappropriate*, because workers should not reveal to clients that they do not believe their statements
C. *appropriate*, because social services are a reward given to cooperative clients
D. *appropriate*, because the worker should inform clients of the consequences of their lack of cooperation

12. Assume that you are counseling an adolescent boy in a juvenile detention center who has been a ringleader in smuggling pot into the center. During your regular interview with this boy, of the following, it would be *advisable* to 12.____
   A. tell him you know that he has been involved in smuggling pot and that you are trying to understand the reasons for his misbehavior
   B. ignore his pot smuggling in order to reassure him that you understand and accept him, even though you do not agree with his standards of behavior
   C. warn him that you have reported his pot smuggling and that he will be punished for his misbehavior
   D. show him that you disagree of his pot smuggling, but assure him that you will not report him for his misbehavior

13. Your unit has received several complaints about a homeless elderly woman living outdoors in various locations in the area. To help determine the need for protective services for this woman, you interview several persons in the neighborhood who are familiar with her, but all are uncooperative or reluctant to give information. Of the following, your BEST approach to these persons is to explain to them that 13.____
   A. you will take legal steps against them if they do not cooperate with you
   B. their cooperation may enable you to help this homeless woman
   C. you need their cooperation to remove this homeless woman from their neighborhood
   D. they will be responsible for any harm that comes to this homeless woman

14. A foster mother complains to the worker that a ten-year-old boy placed with her is overaggressive and unmanageable. The worker, knowing that the boy has been placed unsuccessfully several times before, constantly reassures the foster mother that the boy is improving steadily. For the worker to do this, generally, 14.____
   A. *good practice*, because the foster mother may accept the professional opinion of the worker and keep the boy
   B. *poor practice*, because the foster mother may be discouraged from discussing the boy's problems with the worker
   C. *good practice*, because the foster mother may feel guilty if she gives up the boy when he is improving
   D. *poor practice*, because the boy should not remain with a foster mother who complains about his behavior

15. Assume that, as a worker in the liaison and adjustment unit, you are interviewing a client regarding an adjustment in budget. The client begins to scream at you that she holds you responsible for the decrease in her allowance. Of the following, which is the BEST way for you to handle this situation? 15.____
   A. Attempt to discuss the matter calmly with the client and explain her right to a hearing
   B. Urge the client to appeal and assure her of your support

C. Tell the client that her disorderly behavior will be held against her
D. Tell the client that the reduction is due to red tape and is not your fault

16. As a worker assigned to a juvenile detention center, you are having a counseling interview with a recently admitted boy who is having serious problems in adjusting to confinement in the center. During the interview, the boy frequently interrupts to ask you personal questions. 16.____
Of the following, the BEST way for you to deal with these questions is to
A. tell him in a friendly way that your job is to discuss his problems, not yours
B. try to understand how the questions relate to the boy's own problems and reply with discretion
C. take no notice of the questions and continue with the interview
D. try to win the boy's confidence by answering his questions in detail

17. A worker is interviewing an elderly woman who hesitates to provide necessary information about her finances to determine whether she is eligible for supplementary assistance. She fears that this information will be reported to others and that her neighbors will find out that she is destitute and applying for welfare. 17.____
Of the following, the worker's MOST appropriate response is to
A. tell her that, if she hesitates to give this information, the agency will get it from other sources
B. assure her that this information is kept strictly confidential, and will not be given to unauthorized persons
C. convince her that her application will be turned down unless she provides this information as soon as possible
D. ask for the name and address of her nearest relative and obtain the information from that person

18. You are counseling a couple whose children have been placed in a foster home because of the couple's quarrelling and child neglect. When you interview the wife by herself, she tells you that she knows the husband often cheats on her with other women, but she is too afraid of the husband's temper to tell him how much this hurts her. 18.____
For you to immediately reveal to the husband the wife's unhappiness concerning his cheating is, generally,
A. *good practice*, because it will help the husband to understand why his wife quarrels with him
B. *poor practice*, because information received from the wife should not be given to the husband without her permission
C. *good practice*, because the husband will direct his anger at you rather than at his wife
D. *poor practice*, because the wife may have told you a false story about her husband in order to win your sympathy

19. A worker in an employment eligibility section is beginning a job placement interview with a tall, strongly-built young man. As the man sits down, the worker comments: *I know a big fellow like you wouldn't be interested in any clerical job.* 19.____
For the worker to make such a comment is, generally,
    A. *appropriate*, because it creates an air of familiarity which may put the man at ease
    B. *inappropriate*, because the man may be sensitive about his physical size
    C. *appropriate*, because the worker is using his judgment to help speed up the interview
    D. *inappropriate*, because the man may feel he is being pressured into agreeing with the worker

20. Workers at a juvenile detention center are responsible for establishing constructive relationships with the youths confined to the center in order to help them adjust to detention. 20.____
Of the following, the BEST way for a worker to deal with a youth who acts over-aggressive and hostile is to
    A. take appropriate disciplinary measures
    B. attempt to distract the youth by encouraging him to engage in physical sports
    C. try to discover the real reasons for the youth's hostile behavior
    D. urge the youth to express his anger against the institution instead of *taking it out* on you

21. A worker in a men's shelter is counseling a middle-aged client for alcoholism. During counseling, the client confesses that, many years ago, he had often enjoyed sexually abusing his ten-year-old daughter. The worker tells the client that he personally finds the client's behavior *morally disgusting.* 21.____
For the worker to tell the client this is, generally,
    A. *acceptable counseling practice*, because it may encourage the client to feel guilty about his behavior
    B. *unacceptable counseling practice*, because the client may try to shock the worker by confessing other similar behavior
    C. *acceptable counseling practice*, because *letting off steam* in this manner may relieve tension between the worker and the client
    D. *unacceptable counseling practice*, because the client may hesitate to discuss his behavior frankly with the worker in the future

22. During your discussion with a foster mother who has had a nine-year-old boy in placement for about one month, you are told that the child is disruptive in school and has been unruly and hostile toward the foster family. The boy had been quiet and docile before placement. 22.____
In this situation, it would be MOST appropriate to suggest to the foster mother that
    A. this behavior is normal for a nine-year-old boy
    B. children placed in foster homes usually go through a period of testing their foster parents

C. the child must have picked up these patterns from the foster family
D. this behavior is probably a sign that she is too strict with the boy

23. During an interview in the housing eligibility section, your client, who wants to move to a larger apartment, asks you to decide on a suitable neighborhood for her. 23.____
For you, the worker, to make such a decision for the client would generally be considered
A. *appropriate*, because you can save time and expense by sharing your knowledge of neighborhoods with the client
B. *inappropriate*, because workers should not help clients with this type of decision
C. *appropriate*, because this will help the client to develop confidence in her ability to make decisions
D. *inappropriate*, because the client should be encouraged to accept the responsibility of making this decision

24. Your client, an elderly man left unable to care for himself after a stroke, has been referred for home-attendant services, but insists that he does not need these services. You believe that the man considers this to be an insult to his pride and that he will not allow himself to admit that he needs help. 24.____
Of the following, the MOST appropriate action for you to take is to
A. withdraw the referral for home-attendant services and allow the client to try to take care of himself
B. process the request for home-attendant services on the assumption that the client will soon realize that he cannot care for himself
C. discuss with the client your interpretation of his problem and attempt to persuade him to accept home-attendant services
D. tell the client that he will have no further opportunity to apply for home-attendant services if he does not accept them at this time

25. A worker making a field visit to investigate a complaint of child abuse finds that the parents of the child are a racially mixed couple. The child appears poorly dressed and unruly. 25.____
Of the following, the MOST appropriate approach for the worker to take in this situation is to
A. take the child aside and ask him privately if either of his parents ever mistreats him
B. determine if prejudice against the couple has led them to use the child as a scapegoat
C. question the non-minority parent closely for signs of resentment of the child's mixed parentage
D. observe the relationship between parents and child for indications of abuse by the parents

KEY (CORRECT ANSWERS)

1. A
2. C
3. A
4. B
5. C

6. D
7. C
8. A
9. D
10. A

11. D
12. A
13. B
14. B
15. A

16. B
17. B
18. B
19. D
20. C

21. D
22. B
23. D
24. C
25. D

EXAMINATION SECTION
TEST 1

DIRECTIONS: Each question or incomplete statement is followed by several suggested answers or completions. Select the one that *BEST* answers the question or completes the statement. *PRINT THE LETTER OF THE CORRECT ANSWER IN THE SPACE AT THE RIGHT.*

1. Generally, the *MAIN* reason for using the questioning technique in a case work interview is to 1.____

   A. reveal discrepancies in information given by the client
   B. reinforce your own ideas about the case
   C. obtain necessary factual information about the client
   D. bring out the hidden motives of the client

2. According to a basic case work principle, a worker should "accept" the client, regardless of the client's feelings, attitudes and behavior. This concept of "acceptance" means, most nearly, that the worker 2.____

   A. agrees with what the client says, does, and feels
   B. demonstrates his respect for the client as a human being
   C. has no strong opinions about the client's values
   D. thinks the way the client thinks

3. Before visiting a new client, it is desirable for you to be prepared in advance, when possible. 3.____
   Which one of the following should generally NOT be included in these advance preparations?

   A. *Learning* as much as possible about the client from the medical chart
   B. *Trying* to put yourself in the client' s place
   C. *Recognizing* your own prejudices and stereotypes
   D. *Deciding* on a solution to the client's problems

4. After introducing yourself to a new patient, which one of the following questions generally would be the *MOST* appropriate for you to ask? 4.____

   A. "Do you expect any visitors today?"
   B. "Who is your attending physician?"
   C. "How can I be of help to you?"
   D. "Do you have hospitalization insurance?"

5. In the middle of an interview, a patient makes a statement which seems unclear. Of the following, the *BEST* way to deal with this situation would be for the worker to 5.____

   A. ask the patient to rephrase her statement
   B. rephrase the statement, and ask the patient if that is what she meant
   C. inform the patient that she is not making herself clear
   D. let the patient finish and then try to tie the story together

6. Assume that, at the conclusion of an interview with a client, you have reviewed problems that have been resolved. Generally, the *MOST* appropriate of the following closing actions for you to take would be to 6.____

A. remind the patient to be on time for the next appointment
B. go over specific actions that you and the client will take before the next visit
C. remind the client to take tranquilizers when feeling upset
D. ask the client to think of new problems to discuss during the next visit

7. Which one of the following would be a *MAJOR* responsibility of a worker assigned to the surgery ward? 7.____

A. *Instructing* the nurse about changes in medication for patients
B. *Advising* relatives of the best time to visit patients
C. *Detecting* anxiety of patients due to their medical illness
D. *Recording* the number of visitors received by patients

8. Assume that you have been assigned the case of an eight-year-old child whose parents were both seriously injured in an automobile accident. You realize that this child will have severe problems in the months ahead. 8.____
During the *first* interview, of the following, the *BEST* way to assist the child would be to

A. convince the child of his ability to be brave and grown-up
B. play a competitive game with the child and let him win
C. help the child express his fears and reassure him in accordance with reality
D. tell the child that his problems are not so great as they may seem

9. Assume that one of your clients has many medical and social problems and needs a good deal of supportive case work help. 9.____
Which one of the following approaches would generally be *MOST* appropriate for you to use in order to help this client cope with these problems?

A. *Try* to make the client feel that his problems and situation are unique
B. *Encourage* the client to be realistic about his situation and assure him that you understand and will do everything possible to help him cope
C. *Emphasize* to the client those areas you feel you can work on and those which you can do nothing about
D. *Urge* the client to refrain from taking action on serious matters without asking for your help first

10. Assume that, when you discuss with one of your elderly clients the advisability of applying to the department of socital services for financial assistance, the client becomes extremely upset about the prospect of having to be interviewed by "another stranger." 10.____
Of the following, the *BEST* way to handle this situation would be to

A. explain that applying for financial assistance is something the client must do by herself and for herself
B. offer to accompany the client to social services if necessary, and work with the client toward greater future independence
C. withdraw your suggestion, since the client's emotional health is your primary consideration
D. suggest that the client take a personal friend to the interview to help with difficult questions, if necessary

11. Assume that a newspaper reporter calls and questions you regarding the long wait for treatment in the Emergency Room. Of the following, your *MOST* appropriate response would be to 11.____

    A. advise the reporter that the long wait is caused by an enormous increase in emergency cases
    B. refer the reporter to the director of social work
    C. tell the reporter that your hospital's emergency room is one of the most efficient in the city
    D. refer the reporter to the hospital employee responsible for public relations

12. When a worker interviews a patient whose problem seems to be typical of that of many other patients she has seen, of the following, it would be *MOST* appropriate to 12.____

    A. *attempt* to learn more about the individual circumstances of this patient's situation
    B. *handle* this case the same way as the others were handled
    C. *ask* another worker how she generally handles this type of problem
    D. *reassure* the patient by telling him that many other patients have similar problems

13. A patient without friends or relatives is being discharged from the hospital. He complains to you that his shoes are missing.
Of the following, your *MOST* appropriate response would be to 13.____

    A. advise the patient that this is not a professional concern of yours and suggest that he speak to the ward nurse
    B. advise the patient that he will have to buy a pair of shoes from a nearby shoe store
    C. obtain a pair of shoes for the patient in the hospital clothing room
    D. tell the patient that he probably was not wearing shoes at the time he was admitted

14. The parents of a hospitalized child complain to you that their child is not getting proper nursing care. You have ample opportunity to observe what is happening on the pediatric ward and know that the nurses are extremely conscientious in caring for the children.
Your *initial* interpretation of this complaint should be that, probably, the parents 14.____

    A. are projecting their anxiety about the child's health by criticizing the nurses
    B. are chronic complainers and must be treated accordingly
    C. may actually want to transfer the child to a more conveniently located hospital
    D. are trying to get special treatment for their child from the nurses

15. You are interviewing an unmarried, attractive young female patient who was in an automobile accident and will not be able to walk again. She says to you: "I'll never find a husband now that I'm crippled."
In order to help her express her feelings freely, of the following, your *MOST* appropriate response would be: 15.____

    A. "You feel that no one will marry you because you can't walk."
    B. "Don't be silly. You have your whole life ahead of you."
    C. "That's not necessarily true. You're young and pretty and smart."
    D. "That may be true, but at least you're alive."

16. Assume that you are in your office completing some paperwork. A man enters and introduces himself as a close friend of one of your patients in the terminal cancer ward. He then asks if he can speak with you, and sits down in the chair next to your desk. Of the following, it would be *MOST* appropriate for you to say *FIRST*: 16.___

A. "You probably want to know how your friend is coping with his condition."
B. "You realize, of course, that your friend is dying of cancer."
C. "What would you like to see me about?"
D. "What problem would you like to discuss?"

17. During an interview with a new patient your mind wanders momentarily, and you have missed some details in the patient' s story. Which one of the following would be most appropriate to say *FIRST*, before the patient continues? 17.___

A. "And then what happened?" – so that the patient will think that you were paying attention all along.
B. "Could you rephrase that?" – so that the patient will restate the details without being aware of your inattentiveness.
C. "I'm sorry, I didn't get that, could you repeat that part?" – so that the patient will perceive you as an honest person.
D. "Please continue". – so that the patient will not have to repeat something that was probably unimportant anyway.

18. Assume that one of your clients is telling you about her family situation. All of a sudden, she says: "Two of my kids go to school, and the third, who is seventeen, ..." Then she stops speaking. In this situation, of the following, it would be most appropriate for you to *FIRST* 18.___

A. *state:* "works?"
B. state: "quit school?"
C. *ask:* "What about the third child?"
D. *remain silent* for a few seconds

19. You have just started to interview a new client. He begins by telling you that he has been unemployed for the past three years and is receiving almost as much from welfare as he did when he was working. He continues talking along these lines, and then asks you why anybody would want to work when they can be on the dole and maintain almost the same standard of living. Of the following, your *MOST* appropriate response would be: 19.___

A. "I don't personally approve of living in that manner."
B. "It all depends on a person's values and standards."
C. "If you are happy living like that, it's all right with me."
D. "Let's not discuss that. Let's talk about your medical problems first."

20. During your second interview with a young woman, she asks you to drop all this professional stuff and just be friends. 20.____
Which one of the following would be your appropriate response?

A. "If we were friends, I would probably not be so effective in helping you deal with your problem."
B. "That's O.K. with me, but you would have to be reassigned to a different worker."
C. "That would be impossible under the rules and regulations of our agency."
D. "I really don't think that's appropriate, and I'm a very busy person."

KEY (CORRECT ANSWERS)

1. C
2. B
3. D
4. C
5. A
6. B
7. C
8. C
9. B
10. B
11. D
12. A
13. C
14. A
15. A
16. C
17. C
18. D
19. B
20. A

TEST 2

DIRECTIONS: Each question or incomplete statement is followed by several suggested answers or completions, Select the one that *BEST* answers the question or completes the statement. *PRINT THE LETTER OF THE CORRECT ANSWER IN THE SPACE AT THE RIGHT.*

1. You are interviewing a young man who confides, in you that he is now on probation. In order to help this patient, you decide that it would be desirable to contact his probation officer to obtain additional information. 1._____
Of the following, the BEST way to contact the probation officer would be

   A. *after* the interview, with the patient's consent
   B. *after* the interview, without the patient's consent
   C. *after* the interview, without telling the patient
   D. *during* the interview, with the patient present

2. You introduce yourself to a newly-hospitalized patient and offer to be of assistance if possible. The patient nods that she understands, and begins to discuss her 12-year-old daughter's truancy from school. 2._____
Which one of the following responses would be most appropriate for you to make FIRST?

   A. *I understand your daughter's problem, but can we discuss your problems now?*
   B. *How do you feel this will affect you while you are in the hospital?*
   C. *Did your daughter fail any of her subjects because of her truancy?*
   D. *I have a very large caseload today. Perhaps we can discuss your daughter another time.*

3. You have been interviewing a patient for almost an hour and it is time for your next appointment. As you are about to finish, the patient begins to discuss a new problem. 3._____
In this situation, it would generally be advisable to

   A. close the interview and make another appointment with the patient to discuss this problem
   B. allow the patient to *get things off his chest* before closing the interview
   C. ask the patient why he brought this problem up at the last moment
   D. tell the patient that you cannot discuss this problem because you will be late for your next appointment

4. Assume that you are completing a case involving a deteriorating relationship between the parents of a child who was hospitalized due to an accident caused by the child's father. Since counselling began upon admission of the child, there has been a marked improvement in the relationship between the parents and, in particular, between the child and the father. The child is about to be discharged from the hospital, and you are having an interview with the parents. 4._____
Of the following, according to accepted casework practice, it would be *MOST* appropriate for you to

   A. assure the parents that, as a result of counselling, they are now *ideal* parents
   B. offer a continuation of counselling until the family's adjustment is stable
   C. review with the parents the *do's and don'ts* of being *good* parents
   D. explain to the parents how you helped them solve their problems

5. Assume that one of your clients, an adult male out-patient who has been coming to see you weekly for four months, fails to keep two appointments. The physician informs you that one of this patient's laboratory tests is positive, indicating the urgent need for follow-up medical care. You have sent the patient a telegram, but he has not replied after a reasonable length of time.
According to accepted casework practice, of the following, the *MOST* advisable action for you to take would be to 5.____

A. *contact* a neighbor of the patient and ask the neighbor to persuade the patient to return to the hospital
B. *inform* a member of the patient 's family of the positive; test result and emphasize the urgency of the situation
C. *write* to the patient and explain the dangers of not returning to the hospital for treatment
D. *make* an emergency visit to the patient at home and tell him about the positive test result and the importance of returning to the hospital

6. Assume that you are trying to establish the identity of an elderly woman who was brought to the Emergency Room by the police, who found her on the street, somewhat disoriented. The doctor decides to admit the woman, whose blood pressure is elevated, and who has an open ulcerated wound on her leg. She is very talkative about events long in the past, can't recall where she lives, but keeps speaking of having to *go home to give her sister breakfast*. The police have found that she has a card giving her name and an address which is three blocks from the hospital, but the telephone company has no listing for her.
Of the following, your *MOST* advisable action would be to 6.____

A. ask the hospital security guards to make a visit to the address on the card and tell any relatives of the woman that she is hospitalized
B. have a visiting nurse make a visit to the address and check on the sister's possible need for food and medical attention
C. call the social service exchange to determine whether the woman is known to any agency and what information they may have about her and her sister
D. make a visit to the address on the card in order to obtai more information about the woman

7. You are a worker assigned to the alcoholism clinic. One of your clients appears for an interview in an intoxicated condition. Of the following, your *MOST* appropriate action would be to 7.____

A. discuss the patient's drinking problem with him in no uncertain terms
B. make another appointment and point out to the patient that he cannot be interviewed while intoxicated
C. threaten to close the case and discharge the patient if he does not sober up
D. recommend psychological testing to determine why the patient persists in drinking in spite of counselling

8. As a worker in the family planning clinic, you are counselling an 18-year-old unmarried patient who is pregnant. She is in a state of conflict, because she wants an abortion, but her boyfriend is encouraging her to marry him and bear the child. Of the following, your *MOST* appropriate action would be to 8.____

A. ask the patient why she was careless after receiving guidance from the family planning clinic
B. encourage the patient to make the decision for herself, and Be supportive of her choice
C. stress the positive qualities of her boyfriend, who is offering to marry her
D. determine whether the conflict may derive from the patient's religious upbringing

9. Assume that one of your cases, a woman who has given birth three days ago, is now verbally abusive to the staff, and refuses to see her infant. Of the following, your *MOST* appropriate course of action would be to 9.____

A. scold the woman for her childish behavior
B. attempt to convince the woman that once she sees the baby she will feel much better
C. speak with the woman in an effort to understand her behavior
D. tell the woman that she will be transferred to the psychiatric unit if she does not behave

10. Assume that you are interviewing an unmarried female patient in the Emergency Room. The doctor has just told her that she must be admitted to the hospital on an emergency basis, but she refuses to accept this recommendation because she has three small children, has no one to care for them, and does not want to leave them alone. Of the following, the most appropriate action for you to take *FIRST* would be to 10.____

A. suggest that the patient try to enlist neighbors to help look after the children
B. ask the doctor to admit the children with their mother on an emergency basis
C. try to locate the children's father and ask him to look after the children
D. explain to the patient that it is possible for you to arrange for care of the children

11. Assume that you are assigned to the methadone maintenance clinic. As you are about to finish an interview, your client asks you to lend him ten dollars. Of the following, your most appropriate *FIRST* action would be to 11.____

A. inform the client that it is against hospital policy for a worker to lend money to a patient
B. lend the client the ten dollars
C. suggest that the client borrow the money from a personal friend
D. advise the client to apply to the department of social services for an emergency grant

12. You are interviewing a young unmarried woman who is pregnant, says that she is not sure she can care for her baby properly, and is considering requesting an abortion. Of the following, your *MOST* appropriate response would be: 12.____

A. *What do you think of as proper care for your baby?*
B. *I'm sure you will be an excellent mother.*
C. *Do you know who the father is?*
D. *How long have you been pregnant?*

13. You are interviewing a married patient with two young children with regard to her impending surgery. Suddenly, she asks if you are married. Of the following, the *MOST* appropriate response would be to tell her 13.____

A. whether you are married, and then ask why she wants to know
B. you are not now married, but that you are engaged to be married
C. this is irrelevant, and continue discussing her situation
D. you used to be married, but that you are now divorced

14. You are visiting a new patient on your assigned ward. After introducing yourself and offering to be of assistance, the patient begins to tell you a lengthy story relating to her illness. According to accepted interviewing techniques, of the following, it would be *MOST* appropriate for you to indicate your concern and interest by 14.____

A. briefly commenting or asking questions, indicating that you are grasping the essential points
B. saying nothing, so as not to interrupt the patient's train of thought
C. interrupting frequently to clarify points you do not fully comprehend
D. asking the patient to pause at periodic intervals so that you may proceed to ask structured questions

15. You have been counseling an adult patient on the cancer ward on a weekly basis for about a month and it is now time to decide where the patient will live after being discharged from the hospital. 15.____
According to accepted practice, the *FINAL* decision on this matter should be made by

A. you, the case worker
B. the patient's relatives
C. the patient, with the case worker's help
D. the patient and the doctors

16. Assume that a patient in your caseload asks you for specific advice regarding his unhappy marital situation. In deciding whether to respond to this request, you should generally consider *all* of the following *EXCEPT* 16.____

A. any possible underlying anxiety the patient may have
B. the patient's ability to carry out the advice
C. the seriousness of the patient's situation
D. whether the client will accept or reject your advice

17. According to accepted casework practice, when interviewing a young child it is considered especially important for the worker to closely observe the child's behavior, feelings, and mood, in addition to listening to what the child says, *MAINLY* because such observation should 17.____

A. provide significant diagnostic information about the child
B. help the child feel closer to the worker
C. enable the worker to sense the right time to console the child
D. give the worker clues as to when to humor the child

18. You find it necessary to refer a client for psychiatric help upon discharge. The client consents to this plan, but asks you to omit from your report certain information he has told you in confidence. You feel that the psychiatrist's knowledge of this information would be of great benefit in helping your client. 18.____
For you to go ahead and include this information in your report to the psychiatrist, without the client's consent, would be considered

A. *good practice*, because the psychiatrist will need all available information about the client
B. *bad practice*, because this action would be a breach of confidence
C. *good practice*, because helping the client is the primary goal of case work
D. *bad practice*, because the patient would probably find out eventually that this information was disclosed

19. You are interviewing a woman who has suffered a severe beating from her husband, is obviously upset, and embarrassed about having to relate the details to you. 19.____
Of the following, the *MOST* appropriate way for you to handle this situation would be to

A. insist that she tell you the whole story, including the details
B. postpone discussion of the beating until the woman feels better
C. tell the woman to omit the details for now, and ask her how you can be of help
D. postpone this interview until the husband is available to present his side of the story

20. You are making discharge plans for an alert, 78-year-old retired school teacher who is recovering satisfactorily from a minor operation. One day, when you come to her room, she fails to recognize you and tells you disconnected stories about people she knew in childhood. 20.____
Of the following, the *MOST* appropriate way to handle this changed situation would be to

A. tell the patient she had better *snap out of it*
B. advise the patient that you will return when she starts talking sense
C. confer with the attending physician about this change in the patient's condition
D. suggest to the physician that the discharge plan be changed to recommend admission to a State hospital

KEY (CORRECT ANSWERS)

1.	A	11.	A
2.	B	12.	A
3.	A	13.	A
4.	B	14.	A
5.	D	15.	C
6.	D	16.	D
7.	B	17.	A
8.	B	18.	B
9.	C	19.	C
10.	D	20.	C

EXAMINATION SECTION

TEST 1

DIRECTIONS: Each question or incomplete statement is followed by several suggested answers or completions. Select the one that BEST answers the question or completes the statement. *PRINT THE LETTER OF THE CORRECT ANSWER IN THE SPACE AT THE RIGHT.*

1. One day an elderly man asks you if he can apply for Social Security at the welfare office. 1.____
   Your response should be to
   A. tell him that it is foolish to think he can apply for Social Security at the welfare office
   B. take him back to his apartment because he is too old to be roaming the streets asking questions
   C. explain that Social Security is a federal program and direct him to the nearest Social Security office
   D. call his daughter and tell her that the family should take better care of their father

2. One of your duties is to occasionally visit clients. On one occasion, you visit Mrs. B., who needs assistance in referral of her children for day care so that she may enter a job training program. She has postponed completing the referral. 2.____
   What should you do in this situation?
   A. Tell her that if she doesn't hurry there will be no room at the day care center and the training program will be closed
   B. Make the arrangements and tell Mrs. B. that she should do what you say
   C. Remember that all people who ask for help are not always ready to receive it and continue to allow Mrs. B. to complete the referral by herself
   D. The next time Mrs. B. asks for help, see that she gets it as slowly as possible

3. Assume that you are trying to contact a community group to offer to meet with their representative to explain a new agency policy about intake procedures. 3.____
   In order to "get your message across," you should
   A. write a short concise letter explaining why you want to meet with them and when you will be available
   B. write a short letter stating only that it is important that they contact you in order to arrange a meeting
   C. ask a secretary to help you because you do not really like to write to groups
   D. call the agency rather than write since you know someone there

4. It is necessary for you to call the director of a head start center in order to discuss a training program for teaching aides. The operator asks who you are and what you wish to discuss with the director. 4.____
Your response should be to
   A. tell her that you would rather explain to the director and you want to speak to her immediately
   B. identify yourself, your department, and the nature of your business with the director
   C. hang up and try to call again when another operator is on duty
   D. tell your supervisor that the operator at the head start center is rude and you would rather not be asked to call there again

5. Mr. A. wants her children to go to summer camp. She has receive the request forms, but does not understand all of the questions and you are asked to help her complete them. She comes to the office at the appointed time. 5.____
Of the following, the action you should take is to
   A. tell her she has taken so long that maybe the children will not go to camp
   B. see her as quickly as possible, explain the questions to her, and help her in completing the forms
   C. help her, but tell her she will have to learn to read better and refer her to an evening school
   D. fill out the forms or her by yourself

6. Mrs. B. needs a referral to the cancer clinic. You contact the clinic and make arrangements for her visit. You go to her home to inform her about the time because she has no phone. She thanks you for your help and then offers you a piece of jewelry that appears to be rather expensive. 6.____
Of the following, the action you should take is to
   A. take the gift because you don't want to hurt her feelings
   B. tell her that she is foolish and should spend her money on herself
   C. explain to her that you are pleased with her thoughtfulness, but you are unable to accept the gift
   D. refuse the gift and get someone else to make referrals in the future because she is trying to pay you for your help

7. Mrs. C., a seemingly healthy, intelligent woman whose husband is disabled, and who works part-time, asks for help in getting homemaker services. 7.____
Of the following, the action you should take is to
   A. give Mrs. C. the necessary information and help her get the services
   B. tell Mrs. C. that you do not feel she needs these services since her husband is capable of helping
   C. make note of her request since you do not feel it is urgent
   D. refer her to a caseworker since she obviously needs help in defining her role as a woman

8. When you are interviewing clients, it is important to notice and record how they say what they say—angrily, nervously, or with "body English" —because these signs may 8.____

A. tell you that the client's words are the opposite of what the client feels and you may need to dig to find out what those feelings are
B. be the prelude to violent behavior which no aide is prepared to handle
C. show that the client does not really deserve serious consideration
D. be important later should you be asked to defend what you did for the client

9. You are recording a visit you have made with a client who was angry and abusive to you during the interview. At one point, you lost your temper and said some things that you immediately regretted. You are embarrassed to record that you lost your temper. 9.____
However, it would be desirable to record this MAINLY because
A. you would feel guilty if you did not record it
B your supervisor might hear about it from the client, so it would be better to have it written down from your point of view
C. your supervisor can use the information to help you to improve your skills
D. it is agency policy to write down everything

10. Through one of your clients you learn that a day care program's hours have been extended. You confirm this information with the day care center. 10.____
It is then MOST important for you to
A. make a note of this fact, since it will mean you have to change your schedule in working with the client
B. add this information to your personal resource file so that you can refer other clients to the day dare program
C. inform your supervisor of the new information so that it can be added to the central resource file
D. ignore the information, since your client does not need to have her child in day care for any extra hours

11. You are sent to a meeting of day-care parents to explain the programs of your agency. One of the parents becomes very angry, saying that welfare departments treat people like animals. 11.____
You should remain as calm as possible and say to the parent that
A. he is right, but you have no control over what your agency does
B. he is disrupting the meeting and you have come to explain a program, not to listen to complaints
C. you understand his feelings and that sometimes clients do not get the services they wish as quickly as possible; however, you will do whatever you can to assist him
D. he should call your supervisor tomorrow and make an appointment to discuss his feelings

12. Assume that you receive a telephone call from a very angry father. His daughter took money from his wallet, and he wants the caseworker to control the daughter. He yells, screams, and swears at you. 12.____
What is the BEST way for you to respond?

A. Hang up because you are not responsible for his daughter's actions. He shouldn't scream and swear at you.
B. Remember to be courteous and polite at all times, never losing your temper
C. Transfer the call to the supervisor because you are concerned about the father's unreasonableness and do not want the responsibility of dealing with him
D. Tell him that behavior such as he is demonstrating is the reason his daughter steals from him

13. Mrs. D.'s son, aged 12, has been getting into difficulty in the neighborhood. At a community meeting, she asks your help in finding worthwhile activities for him. It is APPROPRIATE for you to respond to her because 13.____
A. you should have knowledge of the social services available in the neighborhood and the activities they offer
B. you have known Mrs. D. and her family for several years and know how much trouble she has had with her son
C. it is your job to do what the caseworker assigns to you without question
D. you are concerned about impressing Mrs. D with your knowledge

14. Several clients live in your neighborhood. They know that you work for the human resources administration. One day one of them tells you that there is a rumor that another client is pregnant and asks if this is true. You know from a past discussion with the caseworker that this client is pregnant. 14.____
The BEST answer for you to give would be to
A. tell her it is none of her business and if she wants to know, she should ask the caseworker
B. ask her who told her that this client is pregnant
C. explain that anything told to the agency is held in confidence and will not be shared with anyone else
D. tell her you don't know, but will ask when you get back to the office and let her know later

15. The area senior citizens group asks for an agency representative to discuss old-age assistance and new SSI regulations. Your supervisor asks you to attend this meeting; however, you do not wish to go because you really do not feel that you work well with older people. In fact, you don't like them very much. 15.____
What should be your response?
A. Tell the supervisor that you cannot go because you have an appointment with the doctor that day
B. Get another worker to go for you and assume his task while he is gone
C. Explain to your supervisor what problems you have in working with old-age clients
D. Go, because you should do the tasks that are assigned to you according to your job description

16. At a center where you are distributing literature about agency programs, a citizen comes up to you and begins to complain loudly about agency programs. What should be your response? 16.____
    A. Call the police and have the complainer removed from the center
    B. Tell him that you do not make policy; suggest that he go to the office and complain
    C. Remain as calm as possible and ask that he discuss the complaints with you calmly. If necessary, make an appointment with him
    D. Yell at him since this seems to be the way he relates to agency people

17. A community group is having a training program. You are sent to explain agency policy and answer questions. 17.____
    Providing this type of contact between the agency and community groups is PROPER because
    A. you like people and are a good public speaker
    B. it is the responsibility of the agency to cooperate with community groups in order to help the public to be well-informed about agency policy
    C. you were once in the same training program and understand the kind of people who are being trained
    D. once in a while everyone should have the opportunity to speak to a community group

18. While you are assisting in the intake area, a young man who is applying is cooperative but begins to ask you personal questions: your age, where you live, whether you have children, and other similar questions. 18.____
    You are disturbed by these questions, so you should
    A. tell him that agency policy does not allow you to answer personal questions and send him to another intake worker
    B. tell him it is your responsibility to ask questions, not his
    C. tell your supervisor that you do not want to work in intake because clients can get too nosy and you get nervous
    D. avoid answering personal questions and try to get him to return to the purpose of the interview

19. You are assigned to the reception area for the day. A mother arrives in the office with three small children. In a rage, she says that she does not have enough money to feed the children and demands that you find a home for them. 19.____
    The BEST action for you to take should be to
    A. call a security officer and have him remove her and the children from the office
    B. attempt to calm her down by listening to her, attend to the children's needs and call for a supervisor
    C. take the children from her and ask her to leave at once
    D. call the supervisor and security because it is their job to take care of abusive clients

20. Assume that you are interviewing a young unwed mother who has recently arrived in the city from Alabama. She is a likable girl and is very cooperative. However, it is difficult to understand the meaning of her conversation due to her accent and different use of words. 20.____
You would like to establish a good relationship with her, so you should FIRST
   A. suggest that she go to evening school so that she can learn to speak like other people in the city
   B. tell her that you don't understand her sometimes and you would appreciate it if she would explain what she means
   C. take another worker with you on visits to help you in the interview
   D. try to find a worker in the agency who has a similar background and have the case handled by the worker

21. A man being interviewed is entitled to Medicaid, but he refuses to sign up for it because he says he cannot accept any form of welfare. 21.____
Of the following, the BEST course of action for an aide to take FIRST is to
   A. try to discover the reason for his feeling this way
   B. tell him that he should be glad financial help is available
   C. explain that others cannot get help him if he will not help himself
   D. suggest that he speak to someone who is already on Medicaid

22. Of the following, the outcome of an interview by an aide depends MOS heavily on the 22.____
   A. personality of the interviewee
   B. personality of the aide
   C. subject matter of the questions asked
   D. interaction between aide and interviewee

23. Some patients being interviewed are PRIMARILY interested in making a favorable impression. The aide should be aware of the fact that such patients are more likely than other patients to 23.____
   A. try to anticipate the answers the interviewer is looking for
   B. answer all questions openly and frankly
   C. try to assume the role of interviewer
   D. be anxious to get the interview over as quickly as possible

24. The type of interview which an aide usually conducts is substantially different from most interviewing situations in all of the following aspects EXCEPT the 24.____
   A. setting
   B. kinds of clients
   C. techniques employed
   D. kinds of problems

25. During an interview, an aide uses a "leading question." 25.____
This type of question is so-called because it generally
   A. starts a series of questions about one topic
   B. suggests the answer which the aide wants
   C. forms the basis for a following "trick" question
   D. sets, at the beginning, the tone of the interview

KEY (CORRECT ANSWERS)

1. C
2. C
3. A
4. B
5. B

6. C
7. A
8. A
9. C
10. C

11. C
12. B
13. A
14. C
15. C

16. C
17. B
18. D
19. B
20. B

21. A
22. D
23. A
24. C
25. B

TEST 2

DIRECTIONS: Each question or incomplete statement is followed by several suggested answers or completions. Select the one that BEST answers the question or completes the statement. *PRINT THE LETTER OF THE CORRECT ANSWER IN THE SPACE AT THE RIGHT.*

1. Miss Lally is an old-age assistance recipient. Her health is not good and it is important that she have three good meals each day. She follows these instructions except on Friday she refuses to eat meat because of her religious beliefs. She will not even substitute fish. 1.____
You are very concerned about this, so you should
   A. tell your supervisor so that she will go to see Miss Lally and make her eat nourishing meals on Friday
   B. call her doctor and tell him so that he will see her and explain to her that fasting is not good for her health
   C. attempt to understand her value system and accept that it is possible that she is acting in good faith with her own values even though they may be harmful to her health
   D. explain to her how important it is that she eat meat each day in order to be in good health and enjoy the remaining years of her life

2. Theodore is a junkie. Every cent he can get his hands on legally or illegally is used to supply his habit. You are angry because the junkie is destroying himself and his family. You feel that the courts should punish him for his illegal acts. 2.____
Of the following, the BEST action for you to take is to
   A. suggest to your supervisor that the income maintenance center reduce the family grant, taking out his portion
   B. help his wife to find another apartment for her and the children away from him
   C. call the local police to find out why they are doing nothing about this man's activities in the community
   D. reconsider your ideas about punishment, remembering that punishment alone will not help the man to change his behavior

3. You are regularly assigned to taking Sarah Jones and her young son to the clinic. She is a very warm, friendly woman and your relationship with her is good. However, she invited you to come for dinner on Sunday and to go to a school play with her. You would like to accept the invitations because you need weekend activities and you like her. 3.____
What should be your PRIMARY consideration in coming to a decision?
   A. You need friends just as she does, so you should accept the invitations
   B. You are a worker and should not be seen with a client in public places
   C. Decide whether accepting the invitations will help to meet agency needs or will hamper the relationship you are expected to establish
   D. Tell her "no" because it is not a good policy to be on such friendly terms with clients

4. Martha's husband has been arrested in a drug raid and she is extremely anxious. Your supervisor asks that you visit her to determine ways in which the agency may help her. You visit and find her weeping; the house and the children have obviously been neglected. 4.____
The BEST thing for you to do is to
   A. tell her to stop crying and help her to clean the apartment and the children
   B. remind her that her husband has been warned and now has to pay for not listening
   C. listen to her, allowing her to express her feelings of fear, loss, and grief, and reassure her of your concern
   D. listen to her but caution her that she is neglecting the home and children because of her anxiety and you may have to ask your supervisor to remove the children if she doesn't get any better

5. Mrs. Dwight's landlord is very slow in making repairs in her apartment. Each time you see her, she complains about this over and over again, calling her landlord names and threatening to report him to the city. She complains to any agency person she meets. 5.____
Realizing that these complaints are not getting any action, you should
   A. avoid meeting with her because she is annoying
   B. suggest that she see a doctor because she is irrational and should get some help
   C. ask her what she would like to do about the problem and assist her in carrying out her plans
   D. ask the supervisor to see her because you do not have the skills to help her

6. In the day-to-day operations of the human resources administration, which of the following would you consider to be the PRIMARY function of the agency? 6.____
   A. Getting work done to meet city and federal deadlines
   B. Being sure that all of the clients who come to the agency are seen before closing time
   C. Delivering services to those persons who are eligible for assistance
   D. Making sure everyone gets his check on time

7. During the course of an interview you find it is necessary to arrange a special appointment for the client to return for a further interview. After checking your calendar, you tell the client the date she is to come back. The client, however, says she cannot see you on that date because she is to attend a rally at a community center in her neighborhood. 7.____
Of the following, your BEST action should be to
   A. let her know that any other day is an inconvenience to you and remind her that the appointment is for her benefit
   B. forget about the special appointment and try to get along with the information you have
   C. explain to her the need for the appointment and ask when she can meet with you
   D. tell her that since the community center is not city-operated, she must keep her appointment with you

8. In working with community groups, it is important that you be able to define what a community is. 8.____
Of the following definitions, which is the MOST appropriate?
A community
   A. consists of a group of people living fairly close together in a more or less compact territory, who come together in their chief concerns
   B. is a particular section of a city designated on a census tract
   C. is that portion of a city which constitutes an election district
   D. is a section of a city or town in which a particular ethnic group conducts its social, business, and religious life

9. The agency has implemented a new policy regarding the intake procedure. You wish to explain and discuss this policy with as many community groups as possible. You make an initial contact by mail. 9.____
In order to get your message across well, your letter should be
   A. short and as concise as possible explaining why you want to meet with them, and offer several possible times that you will be available
   B. short, explaining only that it is important that the groups contact you in order to arrange a meeting
   C. drafted by the center's secretary and sent to the usual groups
   D put in the usual announcement form in the center's newsletter

10. A group of young welfare mothers want to form an organization that will provide babysitting services for mothers of children who are too young to enroll in a day care center. 10.____
What should be your answer to them?
   A. Tell them to try to get the center to change its policy to include young children
   B. Arrange the time to meet with them to offer as much advice and support as possible, since most communities do need this service
   C. Suggest that it may be better that they spend their time taking care of their own children
   D. Ask a social worker to survey the community to determine if such a service is really needed at this time

11. New regulations have removed the disabled, blind, and old-age assistance cases from the public assistance caseload. Assistance in these categories is given directly by the federal government. A former client has not received his check. The chairman of the senior citizens committee calls and angrily demands that your agency do something in this man's behalf. 11.____
In response, you should
   A. answer politely, explaining that your agency is not concerned about OAA clients
   B. arrange to meet with him in order to discuss the new policy
   C. refer him to the Social Security office covering the area where the client lives
   D. ask that he call again when he is calmer so that you may discuss this matter with him

12. A high school student from the community comes to see you about a homework assignment to write a report on your center. 12.____
The BEST way to help him is to
    A. refer him to a social worker who has daily contact with clients in their homes
    B. contact the boy's teacher and find out why you were not warned of his coming
    C. explain your center's program and answer as many of his questions as you can
    D. give him literature about the welfare system in the city and state

13. Assume that the women's group of the Community Baptist Church has invited you to a Sunday afternoon service to celebrate the tenth anniversary of the pastor. The agency's relationship with the women is good in that they often offer their homes as emergency homes for adult clients. 13.____
What should you do about the invitation?
    A. Do not attend but send them a note congratulating the pastor and explaining that agency personnel do not work on Sundays
    B. Ask a social worker who lives close to the church to go
    C. Accept the invitation if at all possible, attend the service and whatever social hour they may have afterwards
    D. Ignore the invitation since this function has little relationship to your job

14. Suppose that a person you are interviewing becomes angry at some of the questions you have asked, calls you meddlesome and nosy, and states that she will not answer those questions. 14.____
Of the following, which is the BEST action for you to take
    A. Explain the reasons the questions are asked and the importance of the answers
    B. Inform the interviewee that you are only doing your job and advise her that she should answer your questions or leave your office
    C. Report to your supervisor what the interviewee called you and refuse to continue the interview
    D. End the interview and tell the interviewee she will not be serviced by your department

15. Suppose that during the course of an interview the interviewee demands in a very rude way that she be permitted to talk to your supervisor or someone in charge. 15.____
Which of the following is probably the BEST way to handle this situation?
    A. Inform your supervisor of the demand and ask her to speak to the interviewee
    B. Pay no attention to the demands of the interviewee and continue the interview
    C. Report to your supervisor and tell her to get another interviewer for this interviewee
    D. Tell her you are the one "in charge" and that she should talk to you

16. Suppose that a worker asks a client to answer several required but rather personal questions about the family's health history. The client delays and seems embarrassed about giving the answers. 16.____
Of the following, the MOST reasonable response to the client is one which
   A. shows an awareness of the client's efforts to hide something
   B. demonstrates the worker's qualifications for asking such questions
   C. allows this client to be excused from answering the questions
   D. convinces the client that his uneasiness in the situation is understood

17. A representative from a planned parenthood group comes to see you to get information for a community education program. 17.____
You should
   A. check out this group to make sure it is not promoting zero population growth for minority groups
   B. develop a good relationship with him so as to provide better service to clients
   C. make sure they will not encourage unnecessary abortions
   D. refuse to see him

18. A member of a clerical training program is continually late to classes. He explains to you that he has a hard time getting up and asks that you report him on time because he needs to train for a job. 18.____
What should your response be?
   A. Tell him that you get there on time and so should he
   B. Tell him that you do not lie for anyone
   C. Explain that it is your duty to keep accurate records and refer him to a counselor
   D. Tell him that you will cooperate with him but he has to try to do better

19. In a community meeting to explain a new agency policy, you find that the audience has no questions about the policy or your explanations. 19.____
What would be the MOST appropriate response to the silence?
   A. Leave right away before they think of questions
   B. Thank the audience for their attention and assure them that you will be available if there are any questions later
   C. Ask several members in the audience if they understand the new policy
   D. Explain that the audience could not possibly understand all of the policy and they must have questions

20. Assume that you are confronted by an angry member of the public who has not been able to obtain the information he needs from your office. You do not know the answer to his question. 20.____
The BEST thing for you to do would be to
   A. tell him to come back another time, after you have looked up the information
   B. check with your supervisor to find the correct answer

C. tell him to ask in another office, so that you will not lose time looking for the information
D. make up and answer to keep the man satisfied until the right answer is found

KEY (CORRECT ANSWERS)

1.	C	11.	C
2.	D	12.	C
3.	C	13.	C
4.	C	14.	A
5.	C	15.	A
6.	C	16.	D
7.	C	17.	B
8.	A	18.	C
9.	A	19.	B
10.	B	20.	B

READING COMPREHENSION
UNDERSTANDING AND INTERPRETING WRITTEN MATERIAL

EXAMINATION SECTION

TEST 1

DIRECTIONS: Each question or incomplete statement is followed by several suggested answers or completions. Select the one that BEST answers the question or completes the statement. *PRINT THE LETTER OF THE CORRECT ANSWER IN THE SPACE AT THE RIGHT.*

Questions 1-4.

DIRECTIONS: Questions 1 through 4 are to be answered SOLELY on the basis of the information in the following paragraphs.

Some authorities have questioned whether the term *culture of poverty* should be used since *culture* means a design for living which is passed down from generation to generation. The culture of poverty is, however, a very useful concept if it is used with care, with recognition that poverty is a subculture, and with avoidance of the *cookie-cutter* approached. With regard to the individual, the cookie-cutter view assumes that all individuals in a culture turn out exactly alike, as if they were so many cookies. It overlooks the fact that, at least in our urban society, every individual is a member of more than one subculture; and which subculture most strongly influences his response in a given situation depends on the interaction of a great many factors, including his individual make-up and history, the specifics of the various subcultures to which he belongs, and the specifics of the given situation. It is always important to avoid the cookie-cutter view of culture, with regard to the individual and to the culture or subculture involved.

With regard to the culture as a whole, the cookie-cutter concept again assumes homogeneity and consistency. It forgets that within any one culture or subculture there are conflicts and contradictions, and that at any given moment an individual may have to choose, consciously, between conflicting values or patterns. Also, most individuals, in varying degrees, have a dual set of values—those by which they live and those they cherish as best. This point has been made and documented repeatedly about the culture of poverty.

1. The *cookie-cutter* approach assumes that 1.____
   A. members of the same *culture* are all alike
   B. *culture* stays the same from generation to generation
   C. the term *culture* should not be applied to groups who are poor
   D. there are value conflicts within most *cultures*

2. According to the above passage, every person in our cities 2.____
   A. is involved in the conflicts of urban culture
   B. recognizes that poverty is a subculture
   C. lives by those values too which he is exposed
   D. belongs to more than one subculture

3. The above passage emphasizes that a culture is likely to contain within it 3.____
   A. one dominant set of values
   B. a number of contradictions
   C. one subculture to which everyone belongs
   D. members who are exactly alike

4. According to the above passage, individuals are sometimes forced to choose BETWEEN 4.____
   A. cultures
   B. subcultures
   C. different sets of values
   D. a new culture and an old culture

Questions 5-8.

DIRECTIONS: Questions 5 through 8 are to be answered SOLELY on the basis of the following passage.

There are approximately 33 million poor people in the United States; 14.3 million of them are children, 5.3 million are old people, and the remainder are in other categories. Altogether, 6.5 million families live in poverty because the head of household cannot work; they are either too old or too sick or too severely handicapped, or they are widowed or deserted mothers of young children. There are the working poor: the low-paid workers, the workers in seasonal industries, and soldiers with no additional income who are heads of families. There are the underemployed: those who would like full-time jobs but cannot find them, those employees who would like year-round work but lack of opportunity, and those who are employed below their level of training. There are the non-working poor: the older men and women with small retirement incomes and those with no income, the disabled, the physically and mentally handicapped, and the chronically sick.

5. According to the above passage, approximately what percent of the poor people in the United States are children? 5.____
   A. 33
   B. 16
   C. 20
   D. 44

6. According to the above passage, people who work in seasonal industries are LIKELY to be classified as 6.____
   A. working poor
   B. underemployed
   C. non-working poor
   D. low-paid workers

7. According to the above passage, the category of non-working poor includes people who 7.____
   A. receive unemployment insurance
   B. cannot find full-time work
   C. are disabled or mentally handicapped
   D. are soldiers with wives and children

8. According to the above passage, among the underemployed are those who 8.____
   A. can find only part-time work
   B. are looking for their first jobs
   C. are inadequately trained
   D. depend on insufficient retirement incomes

Questions 9-13.

DIRECTIONS: Read the Inter-office Memo below. Then, answer Questions 9 through 13 SOLELY on the basis of the memo.

INTER-OFFICE MEMORANDUM

To: Alma Robinson, Human Resources Aide

From: Frank Shields, Social Worker

I would like to have you help Mr. Edward Tunney, who is trying to raise his two children by himself. He needs to learn to improve the physical care of his children and especially of his daughter Helen, age 9. She is avoided and ridiculed at school because her hair is uncombed, her teeth not properly cleaned, her clothing torn, wrinkled and dirty, as well as shabby and poorly fitted. The teachers and school officials have contacted the Department and the social worker for two years about Helen. She is not able to make friends because of these problems. I have talked to Mr. Tunney about improvements for the child's clothing, hair, and hygiene. He tends to deny these things are problems, but is cooperative, and a second person showing him the importance of better physical care for Helen would be helpful.

Perhaps you could teach Helen how to fix her own hair. She has all the materials. I would also like you to form your own opinion of the sanitary conditions in the home and how they could be improved.

Mr. Tunney is expecting your visit and is willing to talk with you about ways he can help with these problems.

9. In the above memorandum, the Human Resources Aide is being asked to help Mr. Tunney to 9.____
   A. improve the learning habits of his children
   B. enable his children to make friends at school
   C. take responsibility for the upbringing of his children
   D. give attention to the grooming and cleanliness of his children

10. This case was brought to the attention of the social worker by 10.____
   A. government officials
   B. teachers and school officials
   C. the Department
   D. Mr. Tunney

11. In general, Mr. Tunney's attitude with regard to his children could BEST be described as 11.____
   A. interested in correcting the obvious problem, but unable to do so alone
   B. unwilling to follow the advice of those who are trying to help
   C. concerned but unaware of the seriousness of these problems
   D. interested in helping them, but afraid of taking the advice of the social worker

12. Which of the following actions has NOT been suggested as a possible step for the Human Resource Aide to take? 12.____
    A. Help Helen to learn to care for herself by teaching her grooming skills
    B Determine was of improvement gathered on a home visit
    C. Discuss her own views on Helen's problems with school officials
    D. Ask Mr. Tunney in what ways he believes the physical care may be improved

13. According to the above memo, the Human Resources Aide is ESPECIALLY being asked to observe and form her own opinions about 13.____
    A. the relationship between Mr. Tunney and the school officials
    B. Helen's attitude toward her classmates and teacher
    C. the sanitary conditions in the home
    D. the reasons Mr. Tunney is not cooperative with the agency

Questions 14-16.

DIRECTIONS: Questions 14 through 16 are to be answered SOLELY on the basis of the following paragraph.

In social work, professional responsibility and accountability extend to a larger segment of the general community than is true of the older professions which have more limited and more specialized areas of community responsibility and public trust. Advances in knowledge about both the nature of human institutions and the nature of the individual have placed social work in the center of a vast complex of interrelationships. The situations that come to the attention of the social worker, whatever his functions, may be the circumstances of an individual client or of a group or of a community which may or may not be socially sanctioned, and the proposed remedy may be considered desirable or questionable. When there is agreement between the client group and the community on the nature of the problem and on the validity of the proposed remedy, such agreement may lead to the establishment of social institutions. Complication arise when the client or client group, or the community, does not accept the need for change or is not in agreement with the social worker about the direction it should take. The social worker has the obligation to pursue his objective regardless of the difficulties. Even if social work, as it is practiced today, were to achieve the degree of acceptance afforded the older professions, it would still find itself, with every new development, holding unorthodox and not very respectful views on many aspects of personal and social relationships.

14. The MOST accurate of the following statements about the relationship between social work and the other professions is: 14.____
    A. Advances in knowledge have placed social work in a central position among the professions
    B. Although younger, social work has become basic to the older professions in their responsibility and accountability in the community
    C. It is the responsibility of social workers to hold unorthodox views on social relationships
    D. The areas of responsibility of social work within the community are more extensive than those of the older professions

15. When, because of an existing problem, a social worker has advocated a change in a social institution which has been opposed by the community, the social worker should 15.____
   A. attempt to surmount the opposition, continuing to seek to reach his objective
   B. change his position to gain the support of the community
   C. review the position that he has taken to see whether he cannot revise his objective to the point where it may gain community support
   D. work to achieve for his profession the degree of acceptance which is afforded the older professions

16. Of the following, the BEST title for the above paragraph is 16.____
   A. DANGERS OF SOCIAL RESPONSIBILITY
   B. SOCIAL WORK AND THE OLDER PROFESSION COMPARED
   C. SOCIAL WORKERS' RESPONSIBILITY IN SOCIAL CHANGE
   D. UNORTHODOX SOCIAL WORK

Questions 17-19.

DIRECTIONS: Questions 17 through 19 are to be answered SOLELY on the basis of the following paragraphs.

Toward the end of the 19th century, as social work principles and theories took form, areas of conflict between the responsibility of the social worker to the client group and to the status quo of social and economic institutions became highlighted. The lay public's attitude toward the individual poor was one of emphasis on betterment through the development of the individual's capacity for self-maintenance. They hoped to maintain this end both by helping the client to rely on his unused capacities for self-help and by facilitating is access to what were assumed to be the natural sources of help family, relatives, churches, and other charitable associations. Professional social workers were fast becoming aware of the need for social reform. They perceived that traditional methods of help were largely inadequate to cope with the factors that were creating poverty and maladjustment for a large number of the population faster than the charity societies could relieve such problems through individual effort. The critical view, held by social workers, of the character of many social institutions was not shared by other groups in the community who had not reached the same point of awareness about the deficiencies in the functioning of these institutions. Thus, the views of the social worker were beginning to differ, sometimes radically, from the basic views of large sections of the population.

17. The social workers of the late 19th century found themselves in conflict with the status quo CHIEFLY because they 17.____
   A. had become professionalized through the development of a body of theory and principles
   B. became aware that many social ills could not be cured through existing institutions
   C. felt that traditional methods of helping the poor must be expanded regardless of the cost to the public
   D. believed that the right of the individual to be self-determining should be emphasized

18. It was becoming apparent, by the end of the 19th century, that in relation to the needs of the poor, existing social institutions 18.____
   A. did not sufficiently emphasize the ability of the poor to utilize their natural sources of help
   B. were using the proper methods of helping the poor, but were hindered by the work of social workers who had broken with tradition
   C. were no longer capable of meeting the needs of the poor because the causes of poverty had changed
   D. were capable of meeting the needs of the poor, but needed more financial aid from the general public since the number of people in need had increased

19. Social workers at the end of the 19th century may be PROPERLY classified as 19.____
   A. growing in awareness that many social ills could be alleviated through social reform
   B. very perceptive individuals who realized that traditional methods of help were humiliating to the poor
   C. strong advocates of expanding the existing traditional sources of relief
   D. too radical because they favored easing life for the poor at the expense of increased taxation to the public at large

Questions 20-24.

DIRECTIONS: Questions 20 through 24 are to be answered SOLELY on the basis of the following paragraphs.

With the generation gap yawning before us, it is well to remember that 20 years ago teenagers produced a larger proportion of unwedlock births than today, and that the illegitimacy rate among teenagers is lower than among women in their twenties and thirties. In addition, the illegitimacy rate has risen less among teenagers than among older women.

It is helpful to note the difference between illegitimacy rate and illegitimacy ratio. The ratio is the number of illegitimate babies per 1,000 live births. The rate is the number of illegitimate births per 1,000 unmarried women of childbearing age. The ratio talks about babies; the rate talks about mothers. The ratio is useful for planning services, but worse than useless for considering trends since it depends on the age and marital <u>composition</u> of the population, illegitimacy rate, and the fertility of married women. For example, the ratio among girls under 18 is bound to be high in comparison with older women since few are married mothers. However, the illegitimacy rate is relatively low.

20. Of the following, the MOST suitable title for the above passage would be 20.____
   A. THE GENERATION GAP
   B. MORAL STANDARDS AND TEENAGE ILLEGITIMACY RATIO
   C. A COMPARISON OF ILLEGITIMACY RATE AND ILLEGITIMACY RATIO
   D. CAUSES OF HIGH ILLEGITIMACY RATES

21. According to the above passage, which of the following statements is CORRECT? 21.___
The illegitimacy
   A. rate has fallen among women in their thirties
   B. ratio is the number of illegitimate births per 1,000 unmarried women of childbearing age
   C. ratio is partially dependent on the illegitimacy rate
   D. rate is more useful than the ratio for planning services

22. According to the above passage, of the following age groups, the illegitimacy ratio would be expected to be HIGHEST in comparison with the other groups for the group aged 22.___
   A. 17 B. 21 C. 25 D. 29

23. According to the above passage, of the following age groups, the illegitimacy rate would be expected to be LOWEST in comparison with the other groups for the group aged 23.___
   A. 17 B. 21 C. 25 D. 29

24. As used in the above passage, the underlined word *composition* means MOST NEARLY 24.___
   A. essay B. makeup C. security D. happiness

25. A document was published by a public agency and distributed for discussion. The document contained data showing trends in the level of reading among freshmen college students and suggested that the high schools were not investing enough effort in overcoming retardation. It compared the costs of intensifying reading instruction in the secondary schools as compared to costs in colleges for such instruction. 25.___
According to the above statement, it is REASONABLE to conclude that
   A. the document proposed new programs
   B. the college students read better than high school students
   C. some college students need remedial reading
   D. the study was done by a consultant

KEY (CORRECT ANSWERS)

1. A
2. D
3. B
4. C
5. D

6. A
7. C
8. A
9. D
10. B

11. C
12. C
13. C
14. D
15. A

16. C
17. B
18. C
19. A
20. C

21. C
22. A
23. A
24. B
25. C

TEST 2

DIRECTIONS: Each question or incomplete statement is followed by several suggested answers or completions. Select the one that BEST answers the question or completes the statement. *PRINT THE LETTER OF THE CORRECT ANSWER IN THE SPACE AT THE RIGHT.*

Questions 1-4.

DIRECTIONS: Questions 1 through 4 are to be answered SOLELY on the basis of the following paragraph.

Form W-280 provides a uniform standard for estimating family expenses and is used as a basis for determining eligibility for the care of children at public expense. The extent to which legally responsible relatives can pay for the care of a child must be computed. The minimum amount of the payment required from legally responsible relatives shall be 50% of the budget surplus as computed on Form W-281, plus any governmental benefits, such as OASDI benefits, or Railroad Retirement benefits being paid to a family member for the child receiving care or services. Because of the kinds and quantities of services included in the budget schedule (W-280) and because only 50% of the budget surplus is required as payment, no allowances for special needs are made, except for verified payments into civil service pension funds, amounts paid to a garnishee, or amounts paid to another agency for the care of other relatives for whom the relative is legally responsible, or for other such expenses if approval has been granted after Form W-278 has been submitted. In determining the income of the legally responsible relative, income from wages, self-employment, unemployment insurance benefits, and any such portion of governmental benefits as is not specifically designated for children already receiving care is to be included. Should 50% of the family's surplus meet the child care expenses, the case shall not be processed. Form W-279, an agreement to support, shall be signed by the legally responsible relative when 50% of the surplus is $1.00 or more a week.

1. A family is required to sign an agreement to support 1.____
   A. whenever they are legally responsible for the support of the child under care
   B. before any care at public expense is given to the child
   C. when their income surplus is at least $2.00/week
   D. when 50% of their income surplus meets the full needs of the child

2. The reason for allowing a family to deduct only certain specified expenses when computing the amount they are able to contribute to the support of a child being cared for at public expense is that the family 2.____
   A. should not be permitted to have a higher standard of living than the child being cared for
   B. the budget schedule is sufficiently generous and includes an allowance for other unusual expenses
   C. may not be able to verify their extraordinary expenses
   D. may meet other unusual expenses from the remainder of their surplus

3. Mrs. B. wishes to have her daughter, Mary, cared for at public expense. Her income includes her wages and OASDI benefits of $250 a month, of which $50 a month is paid for Mary and $50 a month for another minor member of the family who is already being cared for at public expense. 3.____
In order to determine the amount of Mrs. B.'s budget surplus, it is necessary to consider as income her wages and
   A. $50 of OASDI received for Mary
   B. $150 of the OASDI benefits
   C. $200 of the OASDI benefits
   D. $200 of the OASDI benefits if she is legally responsible for the care of the other child in placement

4. In order to determine a family's ability to contribute to the support of a child, the worker should 4.____
   A. have the legally responsible member sign Form W-279 agreeing to support the child, and then compute the family surplus on W-281 in accordance with public assistance standards
   B. compute the family's income in accordance with the allowance included on Form W-280 and the expenses included on Form W-279 and have Form W-279 signed if necessary
   C. use Form W-278 to work out a budget schedule for the family and compute their surplus on W-281 and then have them sign W-279 if necessary
   D. compute income and expenses on Form W-281, based on Form W-280, and have Form W-279 signed if necessary

Questions 5-10.

DIRECTIONS: Questions 5 through 10 are to be answered SOLELY on the basis of the following passage.

Too often in the past, society has accepted the existing social welfare programs, preferring to tinker with refinements when fundamental reform was in order. It has been a demeaning degrading welfare system in which the instrument of government was wrongfully and ineptly used. It has been a system which has only alienated those forced to benefit from it and demoralized those who had to administer it at the level where the pain was clearly visible.

There is a need to put this nation on a course in which cash benefits, providing a basic level of support, are conferred in such a way as to intrude as little as possible into privacy and self-respect. It is difficult to define a basic level of support, no matter how high or low it might be set. In the end, however, the design is not determined so much by how much is truly adequate for a family to meet all of its needs, but by the resources available to carry out the promise. That may be a harsh fact of life but it is also just that—a fact of life

5. Of the following, the MOST suitable title for the above passage would be 5.____
   A. THE NEED FOR GOVERNMENT CONTROL OF WELFARE
   B. DETERMINING THE BASIC LEVEL OF SUPPORT
   C. THE NEED FOR WELFARE REFORM
   D. THE ELIMINATION OF WELFARE PROGRAMS

6. In the above passage, the author's GREATEST criticism of the welfare system is that it is too 6.____
   A. disrespectful of recipients
   B. expensive to administer
   C. limited by regulations
   D. widespread in application

7. According to the above passage, the BASIC level of support is actually determined by 7.____
   A. how much is required for a family to meet all of its needs
   B. the age of the recipients
   C. how difficult it is to administer the program
   D. the economic resources of the nation

8. In the above passage, the author does NOT argue for 8.____
   A. a work incentive system
   B. a basic level of support
   C. cash benefits
   D. the privacy of recipients

9. As used in the above passage, the underlined word demeaning means MOST NEARLY 9.____
   A. ineffective
   B. expensive
   C. overburdened
   D. humiliating

10. As used in the above passage, the underlined word ineptly means MOST NEARLY 10.____
    A. foolishly
    B. unsuccessfully
    C. unskillfully
    D. unhappily

Questions 11-14.

DIRECTIONS: Questions 11 through 14 are to be answered SOLELY on the basis of the following paragraph.

The employment rate, which counts those unemployed in the sense that they are actively looking for work and unable to find it, gives a relatively superficial index of economic conditions in a community. A better index is the subemployment rate which includes the unemployment rate and also includes those working part-time while they are trying to get full-time work; those heads of households under 65 years of age who earn less than $240 per week working full-time, and those individuals under 65 who are not heads of households and earn less than $224 per week in a full-time job; and an estimate of the males *not counted*, which is a very real concern in ghetto areas.

11. Of the following, the MOST suitable title for the above paragraph would be 11.____
    A. EMPLOYMENT IN THE UNITED STATES
    B. PART-TIME WORKERS AND THE ECONOMY
    C. THE LABOR MARKET AND THE COMMUNITY
    D. TWO INDICATORS OF ECONOMIC CONDITIONS

12. On the basis of the above paragraph, which of the following statements is CORRECT? 12.____
    A. The unemployment rate includes everyone who is not fully employed.
    B. The subemployment rate is higher than the unemployment rate.
    C. The unemployment rate gives a more complete picture of the economic situation than the subemployment rate.
    D. The subemployment rate indicates how many part-time workers are dissatisfied with the number of hours they work per week.

13. As used in the above paragraph, the underlined word superficial means MOST NEARLY 13.____
    A. exaggerated B. official C. surface D. current

14. According to the above paragraph, which of the following is included in the subemployment rate? 14.____
    A. Everyone who is unemployed
    B. All part-time workers
    C. Everyone under 65 who earns less than $220 per week in a full-time job
    D. All heads of households who earn less than $240 per week in a full-time job

Questions 15-16.

DIRECTIONS: Questions 15 and 16 are to be answered SOLELY on the basis of the following paragraphs.

The city's economy has its own dynamics, and there is only so much the government can do to shape it. But that margin is critically important. If the city uses its points of leverage, it can generate a large number of jobs—and good jobs, jobs that lead to advancement.

As a major employer itself, the city can upgrade the jobs it offers and greatly improve its services to the public if it does so. Since highly skilled professionals will always be in short supply, the city must train more paraprofessionals to take over routine tasks. Equally important, it must provide them with a realistic job ladder so they can move on up—nurse's aide to certified nurse, for example, teacher's aide to teacher. The training programs for such upgrading will require a substantial public investment but the cost-benefit return should be excellent.

As a major purchaser of goods and services, the city can stimulate business enterprise in the ghetto. The growth of Blacks and Puerto Rican firms will produce more local jobs; it will also create the kind of managerial talent the ghetto needs.

New kinds of enterprise can be set up. In housing, for example, there is a huge backlog of rehabilitation work to be done and a large pool of unskilled manpower to be trained for it. Corporations can be formed to take over tenements, remodel, and operate them, as in the Brownsville Home Maintenance Program. Grocery cooperatives to bring food prices down are another possibility.

15. According to the above paragraphs, the city is the major employer and by using its capacity it can 15.____
    A. assist unskilled people with talent to move up on the job ladder
    B. create private enterprises that will renew all areas of the city in need of renewal
    C. eliminate poverty in the ghetto areas by selective purchase of goods and services
    D. have no influence on the economy of the city

16. According to the above paragraph, one may REASONABLY conclude that 16.____
    A. the city has no power to influence the job market
    B. a byproduct of strategic purchasing and employment and training practices can be the rehabilitation of housing and the lowering of food prices
    C. highly skilled professions, which are now in short supply, will no longer be needed after paraprofessionals are trained to take over routine jobs
    D. the city's major objective is to bring down food prices

Questions 17-21.

DIRECTIONS: Questions 17 through 21 are to be answered SOLELY on the basis of the following paragraphs.
For each question, there are two statements.
Based on the information in the paragraphs, mark your answer:
A. If only statement is correct;
B. If only statement 2 is correct;
C. If both statements are correct;
D. if the excerpt do not contain sufficient evidence for concluding whether either or both statements are correct.

Upstate, 35% of the AFDC families lived in districts suburban to New York City, 43% in upstate urban districts, and 22% in the rest of upstate. Among white families, 28% resided in suburban districts, 40% in upstate urban districts, and 32% in the rest of upstate. Among non-white families, 43% lived in suburban districts, 47% in upstate urban districts, and 10% in the rest of upstate.

Upstate, 78.7% of the AFDC families resided in SMSA (Standard Metropolitan Statistical Area) counties, including 68.7% of the whites and 90.4% of the non-whites. In Buffalo, 83.3% of the families were non-white; in Rochester, 57.9% were non-whites; in cities of 100,000 to 250,000 (Albany, Syracuse, and Utica), 55.2% were white; and the rest of the upstate urban counties, 86.5% were white.

The two most frequent underlying reasons for a family requiring AFDC were desertion of the father (31.3% of the cases) and *father not married to mother* (30.%). Desertions were proportionately highest among Puerto Rican families (38.6%), compared with 29.4% for Blacks and 23.6% for white families. Unmarried mothers comprised 39.4% of the Black cases, compared with 26.6% for Puerto Ricans and 14.8% for white cases.

White families had substantially higher proportions in the separated and divorce categories than non-whites. When the deserted, separated, and divorced categories are combined, marital breakdown occurred in 59% of the white AFDC families, compared with 52.3% for Puerto Ricans and 44.4% for Blacks.

Substantial ethnic differences existed in the proportions of incapacitated fathers; overall, the rate was 7.5%, but among white families the rate was 14.8%, compared with 9.4% for Puerto Ricans and only 3.0% for Blacks. Families where the father was deceased comprised 5.9% of the AFDC cases.

In New York City, desertion rates (35.3% of all cases) were substantially higher than upstate (18.9%), particularly among white families, as ethnic differences in New York City diminished considerably. Unmarried mother rates closely paralleled the statewide figures.

Incapacity of the father occurred more frequently among white families upstate (17.5%) than among white families in New York City (104%). Deceased fathers were proportionately highest among the New York City Black and Puerto Rican caseload, possibly reflecting fewer remarriage and employment opportunities among these groups in the event of the death of the father.

17. 1. The most frequent underlying reason for a family requiring AFDC was *father not married to mother.* 17.____
    2. Three-fourths of New York State's AFDC families lived in New York City.

18. 1. There were more cases of desertion among AFDC cases upstate than there were of incapacity of the father among white AFDC families upstate. 18.____
    2. There was a higher percentage of marital breakdowns among white AFDC families compared to Puerto Rican for Black families.

19. 1. Desertion of the father accounted for more AFDC cases than all other reasons combined. 19.____
    2. The proportion of incapacitated fathers in Puerto Rican families was higher than the overall rate of incapacitated fathers.

20. 1. Non-white families had substantially higher proportions in the divorced and separated categories than white families. 20.____
    2. Among AFDC families in New York State, there were more Puerto Ricans than Blacks in the combined deserted, separated, and divorced categories

21. 1. In New York City, there was a higher percentage of unmarried mothers among Puerto Rican AFDC families than among white cases. 21.____
    2. Among white families, desertion rates were considerably higher upstate than in New York City.

Questions 22-25.

DIRECTIONS: Questions 22 through 25 are to be answered SOLELY on the basis of the information in the following paragraph.

The question of what material is relevant is not as simple as it might seem. Frequently, material which seems irrelevant to the inexperienced has, because of the common tendency to disguise and distort and misplace one's feelings, considerable significance. It may be necessary to let the client *ramble on* for a while in order to clear the decks, as it were, so that he may get down to things that really are on his mind. On the other hand, with an already disturbed person, it may be important for the interviewer to know when to discourage further elaboration of upsetting material. This is especially the case where the worker would be unable to do anything about it. An inexperienced interviewer might, for instance, be intrigued with the bizarre elaboration of material that the psychotic produces, but further elaboration of this might encourage the client in his instability. A too random discussion may indicate that the interviewee is not certain in what areas the interviewer is prepared to help him, and he may be seeking some direction. Or again, satisfying though it may be for the interviewer to have the interviewee tell him intimate details, such revelations sometimes need to be checked or encouraged only in small doses. An interviewee who has *talked too much* often reveals subsequent anxiety. This is illustrated by the fact that frequently after a *confessional* interview, the interviewee surprises the interviewer by being withdrawn, inarticulate, or hostile, or by breaking the next appointment.

22. Sometimes a client may reveal certain personal information to an interviewer and subsequently may feel anxious about this revelation. 22.____
If, during an interview, a client begins to discuss very personal matters, it would be BEST to
   A. tell the client, in no uncertain terms, that you're not interested in personal details
   B. ignore the client at this point
   C. encourage the client to elaborate further on the details
   D. inform the client that the information seems to be very personal

23. The author indicates that clients with severe psychological disturbances pose an especially difficult problem for the inexperienced interviewer. 23.____
The DIFFICULTY lies in the possibility of the client
   A. becoming physically violent and harming the interviewer
   B. rambling on for a while
   C. revealing irrelevant details which may be followed by cancelled appointments
   D. reverting to an unstable state as a result of interview material

24. An interviewer should be constantly alert to the possibility of obtaining clues from the client as to the problem areas. 24.____
According to the above passage, a client who discusses topics at random may be
   A. unsure of what problems the interviewer can provide help
   B. reluctant to discuss intimate details
   C. trying to impress the interviewer with his knowledge
   D. deciding what relevant material to elaborate on

25. The evaluation of a client's responses may reveal substantial information that may aid the interviewer in assessing the problem areas that are of concern to the client. Responses that seemed irrelevant at the time of the interview may be of significance because 25.____
   A. considerable significance is attached to all irrelevant material
   B. emotional feelings are frequently masked
   C. an initial rambling on is often a prelude to what is actually bothering the client
   D. disturbed clients often reveal subsequent anxiety

KEY (CORRECT ANSWERS)

1.	C	11.	D
2.	D	12.	B
3.	B	13.	C
4.	D	14.	C
5.	C	15.	A
6.	A	16.	B
7.	D	17.	D
8.	A	18.	C
9.	D	19.	B
10.	C	20.	D

21.	A
22.	D
23.	D
24.	A
25.	B

READING COMPREHENSION
UNDERSTANDING AND INTERPRETING WRITTEN MATERIAL

EXAMINATION SECTION
TEST 1

DIRECTIONS: Each question or incomplete statement is followed by several suggested answers or completions. Select the one that BEST answers the question or completes the statement. *PRINT THE LETTER OF THE CORRECT ANSWER IN THE SPACE AT THE RIGHT.*

Questions 1-2.

DIRECTIONS: Questions 1 and 2 are to be answered SOLELY on the basis of the following passage.

The new suburbia that is currently being built does not look much different from the old; there has, however, been an increase in the class and race polarization that has been developing between the suburbs and the cities for several generations now. The suburbs have become the home for an ever larger proportion of working-class, middle-class, and upper-class whites; the cities, for an even larger proportion of poor and non-white people. A great number of cities are 30 to 50 percent non-white in population, with more and larger ghettos than cities have ever had. Now, there is greater urban poverty on the one hand, and stronger suburban opposition to open housing and related policies to solve the cities' problems on the other hand. The urban crisis will worsen; and although there is no shortage of rational solutions, nothing much will be done about the crisis unless white America permits a radical change of public policy and undergoes a miraculous change of attitude towards its cities and their populations.

1. Which of the following statements is IMPLIED by the above passage? 1.____

   A. The percentage of non-whites in the suburbs is increasing.
   B. The policies of suburbanites have contributed to the seriousness of the urban crisis.
   C. The problems of the cities defy rational solutions.
   D. There has been a radical change in the appearance of both suburbia and the cities in the past few years.

2. Of the following, the title which BEST describes the passage's main theme is: 2.____

   A. THE NEW SUBURBIA
   B. URBAN POVERTY
   C. URBAN-SUBURBAN POLARIZATION
   D. WHY AMERICANS WANT TO LIVE IN THE SUBURBS

Questions 3-4.

DIRECTIONS: Questions 3 and 4 are to be answered selecting the BEST interpretation of the following paragraph.

One of the most familiar *type* dichotomies is Jung's introvert versus extrovert. Introverts are motivated by principles, extroverts by expediency; introverts are thinkers, extroverts are doers; and so on. Analysis of the way people react to principle versus expediency situations, however, has demonstrated that most people would have to be described as ambiverts (i.e., they exhibit both introverted and extroverted behavior depending upon the specific situation). Of course, some people behave in a more introverted way than others. A graphic representation of the number of persons exhibiting various degrees of such behavior along a continuum would approximate the familiar bell-shaped curve.

3. A. Extreme extroverts exhibit deviant behavior. 3.____
   B. The bell-shaped curve would indicate that there are slightly more introverts than extroverts.
   C. A continuum is used to determine whether a person is an introvert or an extrovert.
   D. There is really very little difference between an introvert, an extrovert, or an ambivert.

4. A. Extroverts are not thinkers, and introverts are not doers. 4.____
   B. Ambiverts *think* more than they *do.*
   C. Ambiverts outnumber introverts in the general society.
   D. Extroverts possess fewer principles than introverts.

5. The fundamental desires for food, shelter, family, and approval, and their accompanying instinctive forms of behavior, are among the most important forces in human life because they are essential to and directly connected with the preservation and the welfare of the individual as well as of the race. 5.____
   According to this statement,

   A. as long as human beings are permitted to act instinctively, they will act wisely
   B. the instinct for self-preservation makes the individual consider his own welfare rather than that of others
   C. racial and individual welfare depend upon the fundamental desires
   D. the preservation of the race demands that instinctive behavior be modified

6. The growth of our cities, the increasing tendency to move from one part of the country to another, the existence of people of different cultures in the neighborhood, have together made it more and more difficult to secure group recreation as part of informal family and neighborhood life. 6.____
   According to this statement,

   A. the breaking up of family and neighborhood ties discourages new family and neighborhood group recreation
   B. neighborhood recreation no longer forms a significant part of the larger community
   C. the growth of cities crowds out the development of all recreational activities
   D. the non-English-speaking people do not accept new activities easily

7. Sublimation consists in directing some inner urge, arising from a lower psychological level into some channel of interest on a higher psychological level. Pugnaciousness, for example, is directed into some athletic activity involving combat, such as football or boxing, where rules of fair play and the ethics of the game lift the destructive urge for combat into a constructive experience and offer opportunities for the development of character and personality. 7.____

According to this statement,

A. the manner of self-expression may be directed into constructive activities
B. athletic activities such as football and boxing are destructive of character
C. all conscious behavior on high psychological levels indicates the process of sublimation
D. the rules of fair play are inconsistent with pugnaciousness

Questions 8-9.

DIRECTIONS: Questions 8 and 9 are to be answered on the basis of the following passage.

Just why some individuals choose one way of adjusting to their difficulties and others choose other ways is not known. Yet what an individual does when he is thwarted remains a reasonably good key to the understanding of his personality. If his responses to thwart-ings are emotional explosions and irrational excuses, he is tending to live in an unreal world. He may need help to regain the world of reality, the cause-and-effect world recognized by generations of thinkers and scientists. Perhaps he needs encouragement to redouble his efforts. Perhaps, on the other hand, he is striving for the impossible and needs to substitute a worthwhile activity within the range of his abilities. It is the part of wisdom to learn the nature of the world and of oneself in relation to it and to meet each situation as intelligently and as adequately as one can.

8. The title that BEST expresses the idea of this paragraph is 8.____

A. ADJUSTING TO LIFE
B. ESCAPE FROM REALITY
C. THE IMPORTANCE OF PERSONALITY
D. EMOTIONAL CONTROL

9. The writer argues that all should 9.____

A. substitute new activities for old
B. redouble their efforts
C. analyze their relation to the world
D. seek encouragement from others

Questions 10-15.

DIRECTIONS: Questions 10 through 15 are to be answered SOLELY on the basis of the information given in the paragraph below.

The use of role-playing as a training technique was developed during the past decade by social scientists, particularly psychologists, who have been active in training experiments. Originally, this technique was applied by clinical psychologists who discovered that a patient appears to gain understanding of an emotionally disturbing situation when encouraged to act out roles in that situation. As applied in government and business organizations, the purpose of role-playing is to aid employees to understand certain work problems involving interpersonal relations and to enable observers to evaluate various reactions to them. Thus, for example, on the problem of handling grievances, two individuals from the group might be selected to act out extemporaneously the parts of subordinate and supervisor. When this situation is enacted by various pairs among the class and the techniques and results are discussed, the members of the group are presumed to reach conclusions about the most effective means of handling similar situations. Often the use of role reversal, where participants take parts different from their actual work roles, assists individuals to gain more insight into other people's problems and viewpoints. Although role-playing can be a rewarding training device, the trainer must be aware of his responsibilities. If this technique is to be successful, thorough briefing of both actors and observers as to the situation in question, the participants' roles, and what to look for, is essential.

10. The role-playing technique was FIRST used for the purpose of 10.____

A. measuring the effectiveness of training programs
B. training supervisors in business organizations
C. treating emotionally disturbed patients
D. handling employee grievances

11. When role-playing is used in private business as a training device, the CHIEF aim is to 11.____

A. develop better relations between supervisor and subordinate in the handling of grievances
B. come up with a solution to a specific problem that has arisen
C. determine the training needs of the group
D. increase employee understanding of the human relation factors in work situations

12. From the above passage, it is MOST reasonable to conclude that when role-playing is used, it is preferable to have the roles acted out by 12.____

A. only one set of actors
B. no more than two sets of actors
C. several different sets of actors
D. the trainer or trainers of the group

13. Based on the above passage, a trainer using the technique of role reversal in a problem of first-line supervision should assign a senior enforcement agent to play the part of a(n) 13.____

A. enforcement agent
B. senior enforcement agent
C. principal enforcement agent
D. angry citizen

14. It can be inferred from the above passage that a *limitation* of role-play as a training method is that 14.____

A. many work situations do not lend themselves to role-play
B. employees are not experienced enough as actors to play the roles realistically
C. only trainers who have psychological training can use it successfully
D. participants who are observing and not acting do not benefit from it

15. To obtain good results from the use of role-play in training, a trainer should give participants 15.____

A. a minimum of information about the situation so that they can act spontaneously
B. scripts which illustrate the best method for handling the situation
C. a complete explanation of the problem and the roles to be acted out
D. a summary of work problems which involve interpersonal relations

Questions 16-20.

DIRECTIONS: Questions 16 through 20 are to be answered SOLELY on the basis of the following passage.

The dynamics of group behavior may be summed up by saying that the individuals in a group respond to many lines of force arising out of their relationship with every other member of a group and with the group itself. In addition, each member of a group quite naturally brings with him all the things that have been *bugging* him. Then, the situation or the setting in which the group meets, as well as the circumstances related to the formation of the group, are active working forces exerting some *X* influence upon each member of the group. Lastly, all of this kinetic energy is at the control of the person seeking to lead the group into some kind of action. If he is to produce something meaningful with the members of a group, he must utilize this energy, contain it, dissipate it in some fashion, or be faced with difficulty.

This dynamic force inherent in any group can be harnessed by a supervisor with leadership qualities, but it must be controlled. It will not be contained by acting without consultation with group members, by refusing to accept suggestions coming from the group, or by refusing to explain or even give notice of contemplated actions. However, it can be controlled by placing the focus upon the members of the group, rather than upon the supervisor, and depending upon the leader-supervisor to provide as many participative experiences for group members as is commensurate with his own decision-making responsibilities. It is true that this is subordinate-centered leadership, but the supervisor can gain strength through permissive leadership without sacrificing basic responsibilities for effective planning and adequate control of operations.

16. Of the following titles, the one that MOST closely describes the reading selection is 16.____

    A. THE SUPERVISOR WITH DYNAMIC LEADERSHIP POTENTIAL
    B. DISSIPATION OF GROUP ENERGY
    C. CONTROLLING GROUP RELATIONSHIPS
    D. SACRIFICING BASIC RESPONSIBILITIES

17. According to the above passage, the setting in which the group meets 17.____

    A. can readily be modified either in whole or in part
    B. must be made meaningful in some fashion to foster skills development
    C. can provide the sole source of group dynamics
    D. is one of the forces exerting influence on group members

18. According to the above passage, the members of the group 18.____

    A. should control their formation and development
    B. should control the circumstances of their meeting
    C. are influenced by the forces creating the group
    D. dissipate meaningless energy

19. According to the above passage, the effective group leader 19.____

    A. controls the focus of the group
    B. focuses his control over the group
    C. controls group forces by focusing upon group members
    D. focuses the group's forces upon himself

20. According to the above passage, effective leadership consists in 20.___

A. partially compromising decision-making responsibilities
B. partially sacrificing some basic responsibilities
C. sometimes cultivating permissive subordinates
D. providing participation for members of the group consistent with decision-making imperatives

Questions 21-22.

DIRECTIONS: Questions 21 and 22 are to be answered SOLELY on the basis of the following passage.

This country was built on the puritanical belief that honest toil was the foundation of moral rectitude, the cement of society, and the uphill road to progress. Idleness was sin. As a result, we treat free time today as a conditional joy. We permit outselves to relax only as a reward for hard work or as the recreation needed to put us back into shape for the job. Thus, the aimless delightful play of children gives way in adult life to a serious dedication to golf, the game that is so good for business.

21. According to the above passage, during former times in this country respectable work was considered to be MOST NEARLY a 21.___

A. way to improve health
B. form of recreation
C. developer of good character
D. reward for leisure

22. According to the point of view presented in the above passage, it would be MOST reasonable to assume that an employer would consider an employee's vacation to be a time for the employee to 22.___

A. determine his own leisure time priorities
B. loaf and relax
C. learn new recreational skills
D. increase his effectiveness at work

Questions 23-24.

DIRECTIONS: Questions 23 and 24 are to be answered SOLELY on the basis of the following passage.

A recent study revealed some very concrete evidence concerning the relationship between avocations and mental health. A number of well-adjusted persons were surveyed as to the type, number, and duration of their hobbies. The findings were compared to those from a similar survey of mentally disturbed persons. In the well-adjusted group, both the number of hobbies and the intensity with which they were pursued were far greater than that of the mentally disturbed group.

23. According to the above passage, the study showed that 23.____

A. well-adjusted people engage in hobbies more widely and deeply than do mentally disturbed people
B. hobbies, if taken seriously, serve to keep most people mentally well
C. mental patients should be taught hobbies as a part of their therapy
D. the degree of interest in hobbies plays an important role in maintaining good mental health

24. In reference to the study mentioned in the above passage, it is MOST accurate to say that it appears to have 24.____

A. been based on a carefully-structured, complex research design
B. considered the variables of mental health and hobby involvement
C. contained a general definition of mental health
D. given evidence of a causal relationship between hobbies and mental health

25. Across the years, our social sense has decreed that every position of social leadership, every place of influence, every concentration of social power in the hands of an individual, every instrument or agency that has aggregated to itself the power to affect the common welfare, has become by that very fact a social trust that must be administered for the common good. In our moral world, the social obligations of power are real and unescapable. On the basis of this statement, it would be MOST correct to state that 25.____

A. an individual engaged in private enterprise does not have the social responsibility of one who holds public office
B. social leadership carries with it the obligation to administer for the public good
C. in our moral world, the abuse of the power is real and unescapable
D. social leadership depends upon the aggregation of power in the hands of an individual or in an agency that wields concentrated influence

KEY (CORRECT ANSWERS)

1. B
2. C
3. A
4. C
5. C
6. A
7. A
8. A
9. C
10. C
11. D
12. C
13. A
14. A
15. C
16. C
17. D
18. C
19. C
20. D
21. C
22. D
23. A
24. B
25. B

TEST 2

DIRECTIONS: Each question or incomplete statement is followed by several suggested answers or completions. Select the one that BEST answers the question or completes the statement. *PRINT THE LETTER OF THE CORRECT ANSWER IN THE SPACE AT THE RIGHT.*

Questions 1-9.

DIRECTIONS: Questions 1 through 9 are to be answered SOLELY on the basis of the following passage.

The establishment of a procedure whereby the client's rent is paid directly by the Social Service agency has been suggested recently by many people in the Social Service field. It is believed that such a procedure would be advantageous to both the agency and the client. Under the current system, clients often complain that their rent allowances are not for the correct amount. Agencies, in turn, have had to cope with irate landlords who complain that they are not receiving rent checks until much later than their due date.

The proposed new system would involve direct payment of the client's rent by the agency to the landlord. Clients would not receive a monthly rent allowance. Under one possible implementation of such a system, special rent payment offices would be set up in each borough and staffed by Social Service clerical personnel. Each office would handle all work involved in sending out monthly rent payments. Each client would receive monthly notification from the Social Service agency that his rent has been paid. A rent office would be established for every three Social Service centers in each borough. Only in cases where the rental exceeds $350 per month would payment be made and records kept by the Social Service center itself rather than a special rent office. However, clients would continue to make all direct contacts through the Social Service center.

Files in the rent offices would be organized on the basis of client rental. All cases involving monthly rents up to, but not exceeding, $300 would be placed in salmon-colored folders. Cases with rents from $300 to $500 would be placed in buff folders, and those with rents exceeding $500, but less than $750 would be filed in blue folders. If a client's rental changed, he would be required to notify the center as soon as possible so that this information could be brought up-to-date in his folder and the color of his folder changed if necessary. Included in the information needed, in addition to the amount of rent, are the size of the apartment, the type of heat, and the number of flights of stairs to climb if there is no elevator.

Discussion as to whether the same information should be required of clients residing in city projects was resolved with the decision that the identical system of filing and updating of files should apply to such project tenants. The basic problem that might arise from the institution of such a program is that clients would resent being unable to pay their own rent. However, it is likely that such resentment would be only a temporary reaction to change and would disappear after the new system became standard procedure. It has been suggested that this program first be experimented with on a small scale to determine what problems may arise and how the program can be best implemented.

1. According to the above passage, there a number of complaints about the current system of rent payments. Which of the following is a complaint expressed in the passage? 1.____

A. Landlords complain that clients sometimes pay the wrong amount for their rent.
B. Landlords complain that clients sometimes do not pay their rent on time.
C. Clients say that the Social Service agency sometimes does not mail the rent out on time.
D. Landlords say that they sometimes fail to receive a check for the rent.

2. Assume that there are 15 Social Service centers in Manhattan. 2.____
According to the above passage, the number of rent offices that should be established in that borough under the new system is

A. 1 B. 3 C. 5 D. 15

3. According to the above passage, a client under the new system would receive 3.____

A. a rent receipt from the landlord indicating that Social Services has paid the rent
B. nothing since his rent has been paid by Social Services
C. verification from the landlord that the rent was paid
D. notices of rent payment from the Social Service agency

4. According to the above passage, a case record involving a client whose rent has changed from $310 to $540 per month should be changed from a ______ folder to a ______ folder. 4.____

A. blue; salmon-colored B. buff; blue
C. salmon-colored; blue D. yellow; buff

5. According to the above passage, if a client's rental is lowered because of violations in his building, he would be required to notify the 5.____

A. building department B. landlord
C. rent payment office D. Social Service center

6. Which one of the following kinds of information about a rented apartment is NOT mentioned in the above passage as being necessary to include in the client's folder? 6.____
The

A. floor number, if in an apartment house with an elevator
B. rental, if in a city project apartment
C. size of the apartment, if in a two-family house
D. type of heat, if in a city project apartment

7. Assume that the rent payment proposal discussed in the above passage is approved and ready for implementation in the city. 7.____
Which of the following actions is MOST in accordance with the proposal described in the above passage?

A. Change over completely and quickly to the new system to avoid the confusion of having clients under both systems.
B. Establish rent payment offices in all of the existing Social Service centers.
C. Establish one small rent payment office in Manhattan for about six months.
D. Set up an office in each borough and discontinue issuing rent allowances.

8. According to the above passage, it can be inferred that the MOST important drawback of the new system would be that once a program is started clients might feel 8.____

A. they have less independence than they had before
B. unable to cope with problems that mature people should be able to handle
C. too far removed from Social Service personnel to successfully adapt to the new requirements
D. too independent to work with the system

9. The above passage suggests that the proposed rent program be started as a pilot program rather than be instituted immediately throughout the city. 9.____
Of the following possible reasons for a pilot program, the one which is stated in the above passage as the MOST direct reason is that

A. any change made would then be only on a temporary basis
B. difficulties should be determined from small-scale implementation
C. implementation on a wide scale is extremely difficult
D. many clients might resent the new system

Questions 10-14.

DIRECTIONS: Questions 10 through 14 are to be answered SOLELY on the basis of the following passage.

PROCEDURE TO OBTAIN REIMBURSEMENT FROM DEPARTMENT OF HEALTH FOR CARE OF PHYSICALLY HANDICAPPED CHILDREN

Application for reimbursement must be received by the Department of Health within 30 days of the date of hospital admission in order that the Department of Hospitals may be reimbursed from the date of admission. Upon determination that patient is physically handicapped, as defined under Chapter 780 of the State Laws, the ward clerk shall prepare seven copies of Department of Health Form A-1 or A-2, Application and Authorization, and shall submit six copies to the institutional Collections Unit. The ward clerk shall also initiate two copies of Department of Health Form B-1 or B-2, Financial and Social Report, and shall forward them to the institutional Collections Unit for completion of Page 1 and routing to the Social Service Division for completion of the Social Summary on Page 2. Social Service Division shall return Form B-1 or B-2 to the institutional Collections Unit which shall forward one copy of Form B-1 or B-2 and six copies of Form A-1 or A-2 to Central Office Division of Collections for transmission to Bureau of Handicapped Children, Department of Health.

10. According to the above paragraph, the Department of Health will pay for hospital care for 10.____

A. children who are physically handicapped
B. any children who are ward patients
C. physically handicapped adults and children
D. thirty days for eligible children

11. According to the procedure described in the above paragraph, the definition of what constitutes a physical handicap is made by the 11.____

A. attending physician
B. laws of the State
C. Social Service Division
D. ward clerk

12. According to the above paragraph, Form B-1 or B-2 is 12.___

A. a three page form containing detachable pages
B. an authorization form issued by the Department of Hospitals
C. completed by the ward clerk after the Social Summary has been entered
D. sent to the institutional Collections Unit by the Social Service Division

13. According to the above paragraph, after their return by the Social Service Division, the institutional Collections Unit keeps 13.___

A. one copy of Form A-1 or A-2
B. one copy of Form A-1 or A-2 and one copy of Form B-1 or B-2
C. one copy of Form B-1 or B-2
D. no copies of Forms A-1 or A-2 or B-1 or B-2

14. According to the above paragraph, forwarding the *Application and Authorization* to the Department of Health is the responsibility of the 14.___

A. Bureau for Handicapped Children
B. Central Office Division of Collections
C. Institutional Collections Unit
D. Social Service Division

Questions 15-19.

DIRECTIONS: Questions 15 through 19 are to be answered SOLELY on the basis of the following *total annual income adjustment* rules for household income.

The basic annual income is to be calculated by multiplying the total of the current weekly salaries of all adults (age 21 or over) by 52.

Upward and downward adjustments must be made to the basic annual salary to arrive at the *total adjusted annual income* for the household.

UPWARD ADJUSTMENTS

1. Add one-half of total overtime payments in the previous two years.
2. Add that part of the earnings of any minor in the household that exceeded $3,000 in the previous 12 months.

DOWNWARD ADJUSTMENTS

1. Deduct one-third of all educational tuition payments for household members in the previous 12 months.
2. Deduct the expense of going to and from work in excess of $30 per week per household member. This adjustment is made on the basis of the previous 12 months and should be computed for each household member individually for each week in which excess travel expenses were incurred.
3. Deduct that part of child care expenses which exceeded $1,500 in the previous 12 months.

15. In Household A, the husband has a weekly salary of $585 and the wife has just had her salary increased from $390 to $420 per week. In the previous 12 months, each had a paid continuous vacation of four weeks; the husband had to travel to a secondary work location every fourth week. His travel costs during those weeks were $42 per week. In the previous 12 months, they had child care costs of $1,470. What is the TOTAL annual adjusted income for the household? 15.____

A. $52,116 B. $52,104 C. $51,828 D. $51,234

16. In Household B, the husband has a weekly salary of $540. In the past year, he received overtime payments of $255. In the year before that, he received overtime payments of $1,221. His wife has just begun a job with a weekly salary of $330. As a result of this, annual child care expenses will be $2,130. What is the TOTAL annual adjusted income for the household? 16.____

A. $45,240 B. $45,348 C. $45,978 D. $46,824

17. In Household C, the husband has a weekly salary of $555. The wife has a weekly salary of $390. They each had expenses of $33 per week when traveling to and from work in the previous 12 months. The husband had an annual paid vacation of five weeks, and the wife had an annual paid vacation of three weeks in the previous year. There is a daughter in college for whom annual tuition payments of $1,710 were made in the previous 12 months. What is the TOTAL annual adjusted income for the household? 17.____

A. $48,258 B. $48,282 C. $49,140 D. $50,022

18. In Household D, the husband has a weekly salary of $465, the wife has a weekly salary of $330, and an adult daughter has a weekly salary of $285. The husband received overtime payments of $1,890 in the past year. In the year before that, he received no overtime payments. In the past year, there were weekly child care expenses of $210 per week for 47 weeks. What is the TOTAL adjusted annual income for the household? 18.____

A. $57,105 B. $48,735 C. $47,235 D. $46,845

19. In Household E, the husband has a weekly salary of $615. The wife has a weekly salary of $195. During the past year, there were tuition payments of $255 per month for 10 months per year for children in grade school and annual tuition payments of $2,310 for a boy in high school. What is the TOTAL adjusted annual income for the household? 19.____

A. $39,570 B. $39,690 C. $40,500 D. $42,120

Questions 20-22.

DIRECTIONS: Questions 20 through 22 are to be answered SOLELY on the basis of the following paragraph.

Effective December 1, 2004, tenants thereafter admitted to public housing projects shall pay rents in accordance with Schedule DV if they are veterans of the Gulf War, and in accordance with Schedule D if they are not Gulf War veterans. However, all recipients of public assistance shall pay rents in accordance with Schedule DW. Tenants of public housing projects prior to the effective date of this change will continue to pay rent in accordance with Schedule C2 if they are veterans of the Iraqi War or the Gulf War, in accordance with

Schedule C if they are not such veterans, and in accordance with Schedule CW if they receive public assistance and if they are not eligible to use the C2 Schedule. In addition, effective December 1, 2004, when a tenant is accepted for assistance by the Department of Welfare, if such acceptance requires that the tenant pay a new rental as outlined above, the effective date of the new rental is to be the first of the month following the date that the tenant is accepted for assistance by the Department of Welfare instead of the first of the month following the date of application for public assistance.

20. John Jones, a Gulf War veteran, has been living in a public housing project since June 2003. He applied for public assistance on November 15, 2004 and was accepted for public assistance on December 17, 2004. 20.___
If he continues to receive public assistance, his present rent should be based on the ______ Schedule.

A. C2 B. CW C. DV D. DW

21. Jack Smith, who is not a veteran, moves into a public housing project in January 2006. If it should become necessary for him to apply for public assistance on February 10, 2006 and should he be accepted for such assistance on March 5, 2006, the rent that he pays in March 2006 should be based on the ______ Schedule. 21.___

A. C B. CW C. D D. DW

22. John Doe, a veteran of the Iraqi War, was admitted to a public housing project in August 2004. He applied for public assistance on February 1, 2005 and was accepted for such assistance on March 1, 2005. 22.___
On April 1, 2005, his rent should

A. change to the C2 Schedule
B. remain on the C2 Schedule, as previously
C. change to the CW Schedule
D. remain on the CW Schedule, as previously

Questions 23-25.

DIRECTIONS: Questions 23 through 25 are to be answered SOLELY on the basis of the following paragraph.

It has been proposed that an act be passed to provide for family allowances in the form of cash payments, normally to mothers, for children under sixteen years of age. Allowances are supposed to be spent exclusively for the care and education of the children; otherwise, they may be discontinued. They would vary in amount according to the age of the child and would be conditional upon satisfactory school attendance and accomplishment. The allowance would be paid to all families, regardless of means, but income tax exemptions for dependents would be reduced in consequence. The act would also permit the withdrawal of children from school and their entrance into the labor market after completing eighth grade. However, there would be no financial advantage in sending a child to work since the allowances would approximate the child's net earnings. Proponents of this proposal claim as advantages that it would provide social justice by taking into account elements of family need not possible under any normal wage structure system, be simple to administer, encourage an increase in the birth rate, remove unwilling or incapable students from our middle schools, and provide financial aid to poor, large families without the stigma of public welfare.

23. According to the proposal, the one of the following factors which would be LEAST likely to cause a variation in the amount of the allowance to a family or cause a discontinuance of it is 23.____

A. a change in family wealth
B. poor school attendance record of a child
C. a child's being left back
D. use of the allowance money on a hobby of one of the parents

24. The LEAST accurate of the following statements concerning schooling under this proposal is: 24.____

A. A 14-year-old girl attending the 6th grade of elementary school will not be permitted to leave school, even though her school work is unsatisfactory.
B. A poor family will be encouraged to continue the schooling of their 15-year-old twins who are in the junior year of high school.
C. A 14-year-old boy who has been graduated from elementary school, but whose school attendance has been unsatisfactory, will not be permitted to attend high school.
D. The family of a 17-year-old high school senior who is an honor student will not receive an allowance.

25. College attendance of bright children of poor families may be aided by this proposal because 25.____

A. such children will be assured of higher marks
B. families are likely to be smaller and consequently parents will be better able to send their children to college
C. more scholarships are likely to be offered by private colleges as a result of this proposal
D. the financial subsidy granted for a child under 16 may help the family save money towards a college education

KEY (CORRECT ANSWERS)

1. B
2. C
3. D
4. B
5. D

6. A
7. C
8. A
9. B
10. A

11. B
12. D
13. C
14. B
15. A

16. C
17. B
18. B
19. C
20. A

21. C
22. B
23. A
24. C
25. D

PREPARING WRITTEN MATERIAL

PARAGRAPH REARRANGEMENT COMMENTARY

The sentences that follow are in scrambled order. You are to rearrange them in proper order and indicate the letter choice containing the correct answer at the space at the right.

Each group of sentences in this section is actually a paragraph presented in scrambled order. Each sentence in the group has a place in that paragraph; no sentence is to be left out. You are to read each group of sentences and decide upon the best order in which to put the sentences so as to form a well-organized paragraph.

The questions in this section measure the ability to solve a problem when all the facts relevant to its solution are not given.

More specifically, certain positions of responsibility and authority require the employee to discover connection between events sometimes, apparently, unrelated. In order to do this, the employee will find it necessary to correctly infer that unspecified events have probably occurred or are likely to occur. This ability becomes especially important when action must be taken on incomplete information.

Accordingly, these questions require competitors to choose among several suggested alternatives, each of which presents a different sequential arrangement of the events. Competitors must choose the MOST logical of the suggested sequences.

In order to do so, they may be required to draw on general knowledge to infer missing concepts or events that are essential to sequencing the given events. Competitors should be careful to infer only what is essential to the sequence. The plausibility of the wrong alternatives will always require the inclusion of unlikely events or of additional chains of events which are NOT essential to sequencing the given events.

It's very important to remember that you are looking for the best of the four possible choices, and that the best choice of all may not even be one of the answers you're given to choose from.

There is no one right way to solve these problems. Many people have found it helpful to first write out the order of the sentences, as they would have arranged them, on their scrap paper before looking at the possible answers. If their optimum answer is there, this can save them some time. If it isn't, this method can still give insight into solving the problem. Others find it most helpful to just go through each of the possible choices, contrasting each as they go along. You should use whatever method feels comfortable and works for you.

While most of these types of questions are not that difficult, we've added a higher percentage of the difficult type, just to give you more practice. Usually there are only one or two questions on this section that contain such subtle distinctions that you're unable to answer confidently. And you then may find yourself stuck deciding between two possible choices, neither of which you're sure about.

EXAMINATION SECTION

TEST 1

DIRECTIONS: The sentences that follow are in scrambled order. You are to rearrange them in proper order and indicate the letter choice containing the correct answer. *PRINT THE LETTER OF THE CORRECT ANSWER IN THE SPACE AT THE RIGHT.*

1. Below are four statements labeled W, X, Y and Z. 1.____
   W. He was a strict and fanatic drillmaster.
   X. The word is always used in a derogatory sense and generally shows resentment and anger on the part of the user.
   Y. It is from the name of this Frenchman that we derive our English word, martinet.
   Z. Jean Martinet was the Inspector-General of Infantry during the reign of King Louis XIV.

   The PROPER order in which these sentences should be placed in a paragraph is:
   A. X, Z, W, Y B. X, Z, Y, W C. Z, W, Y, X D. Z, Y, W, X

2. In the following paragraph, the sentences, which are numbered, have been jumbled. 2.____
   I. Since then it has undergone changes.
   II. It was incorporated in 1955 under the laws of the State of New York.
   III. Its primary purposes, a cleaner city, has, however, remained the same.
   IV. The Citizens Committee works in cooperation with the Mayor's Inter-departmental Committee for a Clean City. 3.____

   The order in which these sentences should be arranged to form a well-organized paragraph is:
   A. II, IV, I, III B. III, IV, I, II C. IV, II, I, III D. IV, III, II, I

Questions 3-5.

DIRECTIONS: The sentences listed below are part of a meaningful paragraph but they are not given in their proper order. You are to decide what would be the BEST order in which to put the sentences so as to form a well-organized paragraph. Each sentence has a place in the paragraph; there are no extra sentences. You are then to answer Questions 3 through 5 inclusive on the basis of your rearrangements of these scrambled sentences into a properly organized paragraph.

In 1887 some insurance companies organized an Inspection Department to advise their clients on all phases of fire prevention and protection. Probably this has been due to the smaller annual fire losses in Great Britain than in the United States. It tests various fire prevention devices and appliances and determines manufacturing hazards and their safeguards. Fire research began earlier in the United States and is more advanced than in Great Britain. Later they established a laboratory specializing in electrical, mechanical, hydraulic, and chemical fields.

3. When the five sentences are arranged in proper order, the paragraph starts with the sentence which begins 3.____
   A. "In 1887..." B. "Probably this..." C. "It tests..."
   D. "Fire research..." E. "Later they..."

4. In the last sentence listed above, "they" refers to 4.____
   A. the insurance companies
   B. the United States and Great Britain
   C. the Inspection Department
   D. clients
   E. technicians

5. When the above paragraph is properly arranged, it ends with the words 5.____
   A. "...and protection."
   B. "...the United States."
   C. "...their safeguards."
   D. "...in Great Britain."
   E. "...chemical fields."

KEY (CORRECT ANSWERS)

1. C
2. C
3. D
4. A
5. C

TEST 2

DIRECTIONS: In each of the questions numbered I through V, several sentences are given. For each question, choose as your answer the group of number that represents the MOST logical order of these sentences if they were arranged in paragraph form. *PRINT THE LETTER OF THE CORRECT ANSWER IN THE SPACE AT THE RIGHT.*

1. I. It is established when one shows that the landlord has prevented the tenant's enjoyment of his interest in the property leased. 1.____
   II. Constructive eviction is the result of a breach of the covenant of quiet enjoyment implied in all leases.
   III. In some parts of the United States, it is not complete until the tenant vacates within a reasonable time.
   IV. Generally, the acts must be of such serious and permanent character as to deny the tenant the enjoyment of his possessing rights.
   V. In this event, upon abandonment of the premises, the tenant's liability for that ceases.

   The CORRECT answer is:
   A. II, I, IV, III, V B. V, II, III, I, IV
   C. IV, III, I, II, V D. I, III, V, IV, II

2. I. The powerlessness before private and public authorities that is the typical experience of the slum tenant is reminiscent of the situation of blue-collar workers all through the nineteenth century. 2.____
   II. Similarly, in recent years, this chapter of history has been reopened by anti-poverty groups which have attempted to organize slum tenants to enable them to bargain collectively with their landlords about the conditions of their tenancies.
   III. It is familiar history that many of the worker remedied their condition by joining together and presenting their demands collectively.
   IV. Like the workers, tenants are forced by the conditions of modern life into substantial dependence on these who possess great political aid and economic power.
   V. What's more, the very fact of dependence coupled with an absence of education and self-confidence makes them hesitant and unable to stand up for what they need from those in power.

   The CORRECT answer is:
   A. V, IV, I, II, III B. II, III, I, V, IV
   C. III, I, V, IV, II D. I, IV, V, III, II

3. I. A railroad, for example, when not acting as a common carrier may contract away responsibility for its own negligence. 3.____
   II. As to a landlord, however, no decision has been found relating to the legal effect of a clause shifting the statutory duty of repair to the tenant.
   III. The courts have not passed on the validity of clauses relieving the landlord of this duty and liability.
   IV. They have, however, upheld the validity of exculpatory clauses in other types of contracts.

V. Housing regulations impose a duty upon the landlord to maintain leased premises in safe condition.
VI. As another example, a bailee may limit his liability except for gross negligence, willful acts, or fraud.

The CORRECT answer is:

A. II, I, VI, IV, III, V
B. I, III, IV, V, VI, II
C. III, V, I, IV, II, VI
D. V, III, IV, I, VI, II

4. I. Since there are only samples in the building, retail or consumer sales are generally eschewed by mart occupants, and in some instances, rigid controls are maintained to limit entrance to the mart only to those persons engaged in retailing. 4.____
II. Since World War I, in many larger cities, there has developed a new type of property, called the mart building.
III. It can, therefore, be used by wholesalers and jobbers for the display of sample merchandise.
IV. This type of building is most frequently a multi-storied, finished interior property which is a cross between a retail arcade and a loft building.
V. This limitation enables the mart occupants to ship the orders from another location after the retailer or dealer makes his selection from the samples.

The CORRECT answer is:

A. II, IV, III, I, V
B. IV, III, V, I, II
C. I, III, II, IV, V
D. I, IV, II, III, V

5. I. In general, staff-line friction reduces the distinctive contribution of staff personnel. 5.____
II. The conflicts, however, introduce an uncontrolled element into the managerial system.
III. On the other hand, the natural resistance of the line to staff innovations probably usefully restrains over-eager efforts to apply untested procedures on a large scale.
IV. Under such conditions, it is difficult to know when valuable ideas are being sacrificed.
V. The relatively weak position of staff, requiring accommodation to the line, tends to restrict their ability to engage in free, experimental innovation.

The CORRECT answer is:

A. IV, II, III, I, V
B. I, V, III, II, IV
C. V, III, I, II, IV
D. II, I, IV, V, III

KEY (CORRECT ANSWERS)

1. A
2. D
3. D
4. A
5. B

TEST 3

DIRECTIONS: Questions 1 through 4 consist of six sentences which can be arranged in a logical sequence. For each question, select the choice which places the numbered sentences in the MOST logical sequent. *PRINT THE LETTER OF THE CORRECT ANSWER IN THE SPACE AT THE RIGHT.*

1. I. The burden of proof as to each issue is determined before trial and remains upon the same party throughout the trial. 1.____
   II. The jury is at liberty to believe one witness' testimony as against a number of contradictory witnesses.
   III. In a civil case, the party bearing the burden of proof is required to prove his contention by a fair preponderance of the evidence.
   IV. However, it must be noted that a fair preponderance of evidence does not necessarily mean a greater number of witnesses.
   V. The burden of proof is the burden which rests upon one of the parties to an action to persuade the trier of the facts, generally the jury, that a proposition he asserts is true.
   VI. If the evidence is equally balanced, or if it leaves the jury in such doubt as to be unable to decide the controversy either way, judgment must be given against the party upon whom the burden of proof rests.

   The CORRECT answer is:
   A. III, II, V, IV, I, VI
   B. I, II, VI, V, III, IV
   C. III, IV, V, I, II, VI
   D. V, I, III, VI, IV, II

2. I. If a parent is without assets and is unemployed, he cannot be convicted of the crime of non-support of a child. 2.____
   II. The term "sufficient ability" has been held to mean sufficient financial ability.
   III. It does not matter if his unemployment is by choice or unavoidable circumstances.
   IV. If he fails to take any steps at all, he may be liable to prosecution for endangering the welfare of a child.
   V. Under the penal law, a parent is responsible for the support of his minor child only if the parent is "of sufficient ability."
   VI. An indigent parent may meet his obligation by borrowing money or by seeking aid under the provisions of the Social Welfare Law.

   The CORRECT answer is:
   A. VI, I, V, III, II, IV
   B. I, III, V, II, IV, VI
   C. V, II, I, III, VI, IV
   D. I, VI, IV, V, II, III

3. I. Consider, for example, the case of a rabble rouser who urges a group of twenty people to go out and break the windows of a nearby factory. 3.____
   II. Therefore, the law fills the indicated gap with the crime of inciting to riot.
   III. A person is considered guilty of inciting to riot when he urges ten or more persons to engage in tumultuous and violent conduct of a kind likely to create public alarm.
   IV. However, if he has not obtained the cooperation of at least four people, he cannot be charged with unlawful assembly.

V. The charge of inciting to riot was added to the law to cover types of conduct which cannot be classified as either the crime of "riot" or the crime of "unlawful assembly."
VI. If he acquires the acquiescence of at least four of them, he is guilty of unlawful assembly even if the project does not materialize.

The CORRECT answer is:
A. III, V, I, VI, IV, II
B. V, I, IV, VI, II, III
C. III, IV, I, V, II, VI
D. V, I, IV, VI, III, II

4. I. If, however, the rebuttal evidence presents an issue of credibility, it is for the jury to determine whether the presumption has, in fact, been destroyed. 4.____
II. Once sufficient evidence to the contrary is introduced, the presumption disappears from the trial.
III. The effect of a presumption is to place the burden upon the adversary to come forward with evidence to rebut the presumption.
IV. When a presumption is overcome and ceases to exist in the case, the fact or facts which gave rise to the presumption still remain.
V. Whether a presumption has been overcome is ordinarily a question for the court.
VI. Such information may furnish a basis for a logical inference.

The CORRECT answer is:
A. IV, VI, II, V, I, III
B. III, II, V, I, IV, VI
C. V, III, VI, IV, II, I
D. V, IV, I, II, VI, III

KEY (CORRECT ANSWERS)

1. D
2. C
3. A
4. B

EXAMINATION SECTION

TEST 1

DIRECTIONS: Each group of sentences in this section is actually a paragraph presented in scrambled order. Each sentence in the group has a place in that paragraph; no sentence is to be left out. You are to read each group of sentences so as to form a well-organized paragraph. Before trying to answer the questions which follow each group of sentences, jot down the correct order of the sentences. Then answer each of the questions by printing the letter of the correct answer in the space at the right. Remember that you will receive credit only for answers marked.

P. It is unfounded because, while the weak resent the power of the strong, they also respect it.
Q. The hesitancy stems from a concern for public opinion in other countries.
R. The United States has ordinarily been ill at ease in using its military power in support of its interests.
S. The concern is largely unfounded.
T. The roots of American hesitancy are deeply imbedded in the American mind.

1. Which sentence did you put last? 1.____
   A. P B. Q C. R D. S E. T

2. Which sentence did you put after Sentence R? 2.____
   A. P
   B. Q
   C. S
   D. T
   E. None of the above. Sentence R is last.

3. Which sentence did you put before Sentence S? 3.____
   A. P
   B. Q

4. Which sentence did you put before Sentence R? 4.____
   A. P
   B. Q
   C. S
   D. T
   E. None of the above. Sentence R is last.

5. Which sentence did you put fourth?
   A. P B. Q C. R D. S E. T

KEY (CORRECT ANSWERS)

1. A
2. D
3. B
4. E
5. D

TEST 2

DIRECTIONS: Each group of sentences in this section is actually a paragraph presented in scrambled order. Each sentence in the group has a place in that paragraph; no sentence is to be left out. You are to read each group of sentences so as to form a well-organized paragraph. Before trying to answer the questions which follow each group of sentences, jot down the correct order of the sentences. Then answer each of the questions by printing the letter of the correct answer in the space at the right. Remember that you will receive credit only for answers marked.

P. Its lawlessness was virtually non-existent.
Q. The *Old West*, as portrayed in motion pictures, on television, and in books, is completely distorted.
R. It is obvious, therefore, that the *Old West* is falsely presented in mass media solely for commercial purposes.
S. Its heroes, too, were far from heroic.
T. Those who lived in the *Old West* in its final days, or talked to oldtimers, know the truth.

1. Which sentence did you put last? 1.____
   A. P B. Q C. R D. S E. T

2. Which sentence did you put after Sentence Q? 2.____
   A. P
   B. R
   C. S
   D. T
   E. None of the above. Sentence Q is last.

3. Which sentence did you put before Sentence S? 3.____
   A. P
   B. Q
   C. R
   D. T
   E. None of the above. Sentence S is first.

4. Which sentence did you put before Sentence Q? 4.____
   A. P
   B. R
   C. S
   D. T
   E. None of the above. Sentence Q is first.

5. Which sentence did you put after Sentence S? 5.____
   A. P
   B. Q
   C. R
   D. T
   E. None of the above. Sentence S is last.

KEY (CORRECT ANSWERS)

1. C
2. D
3. A
4. E
5. C

TEST 3

DIRECTIONS: Each group of sentences in this section is actually a paragraph presented in scrambled order. Each sentence in the group has a place in that paragraph; no sentence is to be left out. You are to read each group of sentences so as to form a well-organized paragraph. Before trying to answer the questions which follow each group of sentences, jot down the correct order of the sentences. Then answer each of the questions by printing the letter of the correct answer in the space at the right. Remember that you will receive credit only for answers marked.

P. One advertising executive became agitated recently when he suddenly realized that the floors of supermarkets were being unimaginatively used merely to walk on.
Q. Blank spaces, advertising men feel, cry out to be filled with merchandise-hustling messages.
R. He invented a slide projector which projects images on sheets of translucent plastic embedded in supermarket floors.
S. At once, he got to work to correct this unforgiveable oversight.
T. As nature abhors a vacuum, so do advertising men decry blank spaces.

1. Which sentence did you put last? 1.____
   A. P
   B. Q
   C. S
   D. T
   E. None of the above. Sentence R is last.

2. Which sentence did you put third? 2.____
   A. P B. Q C. R D. S E. T

3. Which sentence did you put before Sentence T? 3.____
   A. P
   B. Q
   C. R
   D. T
   E. None of the above. Sentence T is first.

4. Which sentence did you put after Sentence P? 4.____
   A. Q
   B. R
   C. S
   D. T
   E. None of the above. Sentence P is last.

5. Which sentence did you put before Sentence Q? 5.____
   A. P
   B. R
   C. S
   D. T
   E. None of the above. Sentence Q is last.

KEY (CORRECT ANSWERS)

1. E
2. A
3. E
4. C
5. D

TEST 4

DIRECTIONS: Each group of sentences in this section is actually a paragraph presented in scrambled order. Each sentence in the group has a place in that paragraph; no sentence is to be left out. You are to read each group of sentences so as to form a well-organized paragraph. Before trying to answer the questions which follow each group of sentences, jot down the correct order of the sentences. Then answer each of the questions by printing the letter of the correct answer in the space at the right. Remember that you will receive credit only for answers marked.

P. It is estimated that Americans smoked almost a trillion cigarettes in 2020, while they smoked only several hundred million cigars and pipefuls of tobacco.
Q. Originally, they were considered exclusively a *ladies'* smoke.
R. Only in this century did cigarettes become popular in the United States.
S. Far more Americans smoke cigarettes today than smoke cigars and pipes combined.
T. This was not always the case, however.

1. Which sentence did you put first? 1.____
   A. P B. Q C. R D. S E. T

2. Which sentence did you put after Sentence Q? 2.____
   A. P
   B. R
   C. S
   D. T
   E. None of the above. Sentence Q is last.

3. Which sentence did you put before Sentence T? 3.____
   A. P
   B. Q
   C. R
   D. S
   E. None of the above. Sentence T is last.

4. Which sentence did you put after Sentence R? 4.____
   A. P
   B. Q
   C. S
   D. T
   E. None of the above. Sentence R is last.

5. Which sentence did you put before Sentence R? 5.____
   A. P
   B. Q
   C. S
   D. T
   E. None of the above. Sentence R is first.

KEY (CORRECT ANSWERS)

1. D
2. E
3. A
4. B
5. D

TEST 5

DIRECTIONS: Each group of sentences in this section is actually a paragraph presented in scrambled order. Each sentence in the group has a place in that paragraph; no sentence is to be left out. You are to read each group of sentences so as to form a well-organized paragraph. Before trying to answer the questions which follow each group of sentences, jot down the correct order of the sentences. Then answer each of the questions by printing the letter of the correct answer in the space at the right. Remember that you will receive credit only for answers marked.

P. A *megagram*, or a million *grams*, is, therefore, equal to 2.205 pounds.
Q. A *gram* is equivalent to 1/28.35 ounces.
R. The fundamental unit of mass in the metric system is the *gram*.
S. A *kilogram*, or a thousand *grams*, is equal to 2.205 pounds.
T. *Gram* is derived from the late Greek, *gramma*, meaning a *small weight*.

1. Which sentence did you put after Sentence S? 1.____
   A. P
   B. Q
   C. R
   D. T
   E. None of the above. Sentence S is last.

2. Which sentence did you put before Sentence T? 2.____
   A. P
   B. Q
   C. R
   D. S
   E. None of the above. Sentence T is first.

3. Which sentence did you put after Sentence Q? 3.____
   A. P
   B. R
   C. S
   D. T
   E. None of the above. Sentence Q is last.

4. Which sentence did you put before Sentence R? 4.____
   A. P
   B. Q
   C. S
   D. T
   E. None of the above. Sentence R is first.

5. Which sentence did you put after Sentence T? 5.____
   A. P
   B. Q
   C. R
   D. S
   E. None of the above. Sentence T is last.

KEY (CORRECT ANSWERS)

1. A
2. C
3. C
4. E
5. B

PREPARING WRITTEN MATERIAL

EXAMINATION SECTION

TEST 1

DIRECTIONS: The following groups of sentences need to be arranged in an order that makes sense. Select the letter preceding the sequence that represents the BEST sentence order. *PRINT THE LETTER OF THE CORRECT ANSWER IN THE SPACE AT THE RIGHT.*

1. I. A large Naval station on Alameda Island, near Oakland, held many warships in port, and the War Department was worried that if the bridge were to be blown up by the enemy, passage to and from the bay would be hopelessly blocked. 1.____
   II. Though many skeptics were opposed to the idea of building such an enormous bridge, the most vocal opposition came from a surprising source: the United States War Department.
   III. The War Department's concerns led to a showdown at San Francisco City Hall between Strauss and the Secretary of War, who demanded to know what would happen if a military enemy blew up the bridge.
   IV. In 1933, by submitting a construction cost estimate of $17 million, an engineer named Joseph Strauss won the contract to build the Golden Gate Bridge of San Francisco, which would then become one of the world's largest bridges.
   V. Strauss quickly ended the debate by explaining that the Golden Gate Bridge was to be a suspension bridge, whose roadway would hang in the air from cables strung between two huge towers, and would immediately sink into three hundred feet of water if it were destroyed.

   The BEST order is:
   A. II, III, I, IV, V B. I, II, III, V, IV C. IV, II, I, III, V D. IV, I, III, V, II

2. I. Plastic surgeons have already begun to use virtual reality to map out the complex nerve and tissue structures of a particular patient's face, in order to prepare for delicate surgery. 2.____
   II. A virtual reality program responds to these movements by adjusting the images that a person sees on a screen or through goggles, thereby creating an "interactive" world in which a person can see and touch three-dimensional graphic objects.
   III. No more than a computer program that is designed to build and display graphic images, the virtual reality program takes graphic programs a step further by sensing a person's head and body movements.
   IV. The computer technology known as virtual reality, now in its very first stages of development, is already revolutionizing some aspects of contemporary life.
   V. Virtual reality computers are also being used by the space program, most recently to simulate conditions for the astronauts who were launched on a repair mission to the Hubble telescope.

The BEST order is:

A. IV, II, I, V, III B. III, I, V, II, IV C. IV, III, II, I, V D. III, I, II, IV, V

3. I. Before you plant anything, the soil in your plant bed should be carefully raked level, a small section at a time, and any clods or rocks that can't be broken up should be removed. 3.____

II. Your plant should be placed in a hole that will position it at the same level it was at the nursery, and a small indentation should be pressed into the soil around the plant in order to hold water near its roots.

III. Before placing the plant in the soil, lightly separate any roots that may have been matted together in the container, cutting away any thick masses that can't be separated, so that the remaining roots will be able to grow outward.

IV. After the bed is ready, remove your plant from its container by turning it upside down and tapping or pushing on the bottom —never remove it by pulling on the plant.

V. When you bring home a small plant in an individual container from the nursery, there are several things to remember while preparing to plant it in your own garden.

The BEST order is:

A. V, IV, III, II, I B. V, II, IV, III, II C. I, IV, II, III, V D. I, IV, V, II, III

4. I. The motte and its tower were usually built first, so that sentries could use it as a lookout to warn the castle workers of any danger that might approach the castle. 4.____

II. Though the moat and palisade offered the bailey a good deal of protection, it was linked to the motte by a set of stairs that led to a retractable drawbridge at the motte's gate, to enable people to evacuate onto the motte in case of an attack.

III. The motte of these early castles was a fortified hill, sometimes as high as one hundred feet, on which stood a palisade and tower.

IV. The bailey was a clear, level spot below the motte, also enclosed by a palisade, which in turn was surrounded by a large trench or moat.

V. The earliest castles built in Europe were not the magnificent stone giants that still tower over much of the European landscape, but simpler wooden constructions called motte-and-bailey castles.

The BEST order is:

A. V, III, I, IV, II B. V, IV, I, II, III C. I, IV, III, II, V D. I, III, II, IV, V

5. I. If an infant is left alone or abandoned for a short while, its immediate response is to cry loudly, accompanying its screams with aggressive flailing of its legs and limbs. 5.____

II. If a child has been abandoned for a longer period of time, it becomes completely still and quiet, as if realizing that now its only chance for survival is to shut its mouth and remain motionless.

III. Along with their intense fear of the dark, the crying behavior of human infants offers insights into how prehistoric newborn children might have evolved instincts that would prevent them from becoming victims of predators.

IV. This behavior often surprises people who enter a hospital's maternity ward for the first time and encounter total silence from a roomful of infants.
V. This violent screaming response is quite different from an infant's cries of discomfort or hunger, and seems to serve as either the child's first line of defense against an unwanted intruder, or a desperate attempt to communicate its position to the mother.

The BEST order is:
A. III, II, IV, I, V B. III, I, V, II, IV C. I, V, IV, II, III D. II, IV, I, V, III

6. I. When two cats meet who are strangers, their first actions and gestures determine who the "dominant" cat will be, at least for the time being. 6.____
II. Unlike dogs, cats are typically a solitary animal species who avoid social interaction, but they do display specific social responses to each other upon meeting.
III. This is unlikely, however; before such a point of open hostility is reached, one of the cats will usually take the "submissive" position of crouching down while looking away from the other dat.
IV. If a cat desires dominance or sees the other cat as a threat to its territory, it will stare directly at the intruder with a lowered tail.
V. If the other cat responds with a similar gesture, or with the strong defensive posture of an arched back, laid-back ears and raised tail, a fight or chase is likely if neither cat gives in.

The BEST order is:
A. IV, II, I, V, III B. I, II, IV, V, III C. I, IV, V, III, II D. II, I, IV, V, III

7. I. A star or planet's gravitational force can best be explained in this way: anything passing through this "dent" in space will veer toward the star or planet as if it were rolling into a hole. 7.____
II. Objects that are massive or heavy, such as stars or planets, "sink" into this surface, creating a sort of dent or concavity in the surrounding space.
III. Black holes, the most massive objects known to exist in space, create dents so large and deep that the space surrounding them actually folds in on itself, preventing anything that falls in —even light —from ever escaping again.
IV. The sort of dent a star or planet makes depends on how massive it is; planets generally have weak gravitational pulls, but stars, which are larger and heavier, make a bigger "dent" that will attract more matter.
V. In outer space, the force of gravity works as if the surrounding space is a soft, flat surface.

The BEST order is:
A. III, V, II, I, IV B. III, IV, I, V, II C. V, II, I, IV, III D. I, V, II, IV, III

8. I. Eventually, the society of Kyoto gave the world one of its first and greatest novels when Japan's most promising writer, Lady Murasaki Shikibu, wrote her chronicle of Kyoto's society, *The Tale of Genji*, which preceded the first European novels by more than 500 years. 8.____
II. The society of Kyoto was dedicated to the pleasures of art; the courtiers experimented with new and colorful methods of sculpture, painting, writing, decorative gardening, and even making clothes.

III. Japanese culture began under the powerful authority of Chinese Buddhism, which influenced every aspect of Japanese life from religion to politics and art.
IV. This new, vibrant culture was so sophisticated that all the people in Kyoto's imperial court considered themselves poets, and the line between life and art hardly existed —lovers corresponded entirely through written verses, and even government officials communicated by writing poems to each other.
V. In the eighth century, when the emperor established the town of Kyoto as the capital of the Japanese empire, Japanese society began to develop its own distinctive style.

The BEST order is:
A. V, II, IV, I, III B. II, I, V, IV, III C. V, III, IV, I, II D. III, V, II, IV, I

9. I. Instead of wheels, the HSST uses two sets of magnets, one which sits on the track, and another that is carried by the train; these magnets generate an identical magnetic field which forces the two sets apart. 9.____
II. In the last few decades, railway travel has become less popular throughout the world, because it is much slower than travel by airplane, and not much less expensive.
III. The HSST's designers say that the train can take passengers from one town to another as quickly as a jet plane —while consuming less than half the energy.
IV. This repellent effect is strong enough to lift the entire train above the trackway, and the train, literally traveling on air, rockets along at speeds of up to 300 miles per hour.
V. The revolutionary technology of magnetic levitation, currently being tested by Japan's experimental HSST (High Speed Surface Transport), may yet bring passenger trains back from the dead.

The BEST order is:
A. II, V, I, IV, III B. II, I, IV, III, V C. V, II, III, I, IV D. V, I, III, IV, II

10. I. When European countries first began to colonize the African continent, their impression of the African people was of a vast group of loosely organized tribal societies, without any great centralized source of power or wealth. 10.____
II. The legend of Timbuktu persisted until the nineteenth century, when a French adventurer visited Timbuktu and found that raids by neighboring tribesmen had made the city a shadow of its former self.
III. In the fifteenth century, when the stories of travelers who had traveled Africa's Sudan region began circulating around Europe, this impression began to change.
IV. In 1470, an Italian merchant named Benedetto Dei traveled to Timbuktu and confirmed these rumors, describing a thriving metropolis where rich and poor people worshipped together in the city's many ornate mosques — there was even a university in Timbuktu, much like its European counterparts, where African scholars pursued their studies in the arts and sciences.

V. The travelers' legends told of an enormous city in the western Sudan, Timbuktu, where the streets were crowded with goods brought by faraway caravans, and where there was a stone palace as large as any in Europe.

The BEST order is:

A. III, V, I, IV, II B. I, II, IV, III, V C. I, III, V, IV, II D. II, I, III, IV, V

11. I. Also, our reference points in sighting the moon make us believe that its size is changing; when the moon is rising through the trees, it seems huge, because our brains unconsciously compare the size of the moon with the size of the trees in the foreground. 11.____

II. To most people, the sky itself appears more distant at the horizon than directly overhead, and if the moon's size—which remains constant—is projected from the horizon, the apparent distance of the horizon makes the moon look bigger.

III. Up higher in the sky, the moon is set against tiny stars in the background, which will make the moon seem smaller.

IV. People often wonder why the moon becomes bigger when it approaches the horizon, but most scientists agree that this is a complicated optical illusion, produced by at least three factors.

V. The moon illusion may also be partially explained by a phenomenon that has nothing to do with errors in our perception—light that enters the earth's atmosphere is sometimes refracted, and so the atmosphere may act as a kind of magnifying glass for the moon's image.

The BEST order is:

A. IV, III, V, II, I B. IV, II, I, III, V C. V, II, I, III, IV D. II, I, III, IV, V

12. I. When the Native Americans were introduced to the horses used by white explorers, they were amazed at their new alternative—here was an animal that was strong and swift, would patiently carry a person or other loads on its back, and they later discovered, was right at home on the plains. 12.____

II. Before the arrival of European explorers to North America, the natives of the American plains used large dogs to carry their travois-long lodgepoles loaded with clothing, gear, and food.

III. These horses, it is now known, were not really strangers to North America; the very first horses originated here, on this continent, tens of thousands of years ago, and migrated into Asia across the Bering Land Bridge, a strip of land that used to link our continent with the Eastern world.

IV. At first, the natives knew so little about horses that at least one tribe tried to feed their new animals pieces of dried meat and animal fat, and were surprised when the horses turned their heads away and began to eat the grass of the prairie.

V. The American horse eventually became extinct, but its Asian cousins were reintroduced to the New World when the European explorers brought them to live among the Native Americans.

The BEST order is:

A. II, I, IV, III, V B. II, IV, I, III, V C. I, II, IV, III, V D. I, III, V, II, IV

13. I. The dress worn by the dancer is believed to have been adorned in the past by shells which would strike each other as the dancer performed, creating a lovely sound. 13.____
II. Today's jingle-dress is decorated with the tin lids of snuff cans, which are rolled into cones and sewn onto the dress,
III. During the jingle-dress dance, the dancer must blend complicated footwork with a series of gentle hos that cause the cones to jingle in rhythm to a drumbeat.
IV. When contemporary Native American tribes meet for a pow-wow, one of the most popular ceremonies to take place is the women's jingle-dress dance.
V. Besides being more readily available than shells, the lids are thought by many dancers to create a softer, more subtle sound.

The BEST order is:

A. II, IV, V, I, III B. IV, II, I, III, V C. II, I, III, V, IV D. IV, I, II, V, III

14. I. If a homeowner lives where seasonal climates are extreme, deciduous shade trees—which will drop their leaves in the winter and allow sunlight to pass through the windows—should be planted near the southern exposure in order to keep the house cool during the summer. 14.____
II. This trajectory is shorter and lower in the sky than at any other time of year during the winter, when a house most requires heating; the northern-facing parts of a house do not receive any direct sunlight at all.
III. In designing an energy-efficient house, especially in colder climates, it is important to remember that most of the house's windows should face south.
IV. Though the sun always rises in the east and sets in the west, the sun of the northern hemisphere is permanently situated in the southern portion of the sky.
V. The explanation for why so many architects and builders want this "southern exposure" is related to the path of the sun in the sky.

The BEST order is:

A. III, I, V, IV, II B. III, V, IV, II, I C. I, III, IV, II, V D. I, II, V, IV, III

15. I. His journeying lasted twenty-four years and took him over an estimated 75,000 miles, a distance that would not be surpassed by anyone other than Magellan—who sailed around the world—for another six hundred years. 15.____
II. Perhaps the most far-flung of these lesser-known travelers was Ibn Batuta, an African Moslem who left his birthplace of Tangier in the summer of 1325.
III. Ibn Batuta traveled all over Africa and Asia, from Niger to Peking, and to the islands of Maldive and Indonesia.
IV. However, a few explorers of the Eastern world logged enough miles and adventures to make Marco Polo's voyage look like an evening stroll.
V. In America, the most well-known of the Old World's explorers are usually Europeans such as Marco Polo, the Italian who brought many elements of Chinese culture to the Western world.

The BEST order is:

A. V, IV, II, III, I B. V, IV, III, II, I C. III, II, I, IV, V D. II, III, I, IV, V

16. I. In the rainforests of South America, a rare species of frog practices a reproductive method that is entirely different from this standard process. 16.____
    II. She will eventually carry each of the tadpoles up into the canopy and drop each into its own little pool, where it will be easy to locate and safe from most predators.
    III. After fertilization, the female of the species, who lives almost entirely on the forest floor, lays between 2 and 16 eggs among the leaf litter at the base of a tree, and stands watch over these eggs until they hatch.
    IV. Most frogs are pond-dwellers who are able to deposit hundreds of eggs in the water and then leave them alone, knowing that enough eggs have been laid to insure the survival of some of their offspring.
    V. Once the tadpoles emerge, the female backs in among them, and a tadpole will wriggle onto her back to be carried high into the forest canopy, where the female will deposit it in a little pool of water cupped in the leaf of a plant.

    The BEST order is:
    A. I, IV, III, II, V B. I, III, V, II, IV C. IV, III, II, V, I D. IV, I, III, V, II

17. I. Eratosthenes had heard from travelers that at exactly noon on June 21, in the ancient city of Aswan, Egypt, the sun cast no shadow in a well, which meant that the sun must be directly overhead. 17.____
    II. He knew the sun always cast a shadow in Alexandria, and so he figured that if he could measure the length of an Alexandria shadow at the time when there was no shadow in Aswan, he could calculate the angle of the sun, and therefore the circumference of the earth.
    III. The evidence for a round earth was not new in 1492; in fact, Eratosthenes, an Alexandrian geographer who lived nearly sixteen centuries before Columbus's voyage (275-195 B.C.), actually developed a method for calculating the circumference of the earth that is still in use today.
    IV. Eratosthenes's method was correct, but his result—28,700 miles—was about 15 percent too high, probably because of the inaccurate ancient methods of keeping time, and because Aswan was not due south of Alexandria, as Eratosthenes had believed.
    V. When Christopher Columbus sailed across the Atlantic Ocean for the first time in 1492, there were still some people in the world who ignored scientific evidence and believed that the earth was flat, rather than round.

    The BEST order is:
    A. I, II, V, III, IV B. V, III, IV, I, II C. V, III, I, II, IV D. III, V, I, II, IV

18. I. The first name for the child is considered a trial naming, often impersonal and neutral, such as the Ngoni name *Chabwera*, meaning "it has arrived." 18.____
    II. This sort of name is not due to any parental indifference to the child, but is a kind of silent recognition of Africa's sometimes high infant death rate; most parents ease the pain of losing a child with the belief that it is not really a person until it has been given a final name.
    III. In many tribal African societies, families often give two different names to their children, at different periods in time.
    IV. After the trial naming period has subsided and it is clear that the child will survive, the parents choose a final name for the child, an act that symbolically completes the act of birth.

V. In fact, some African first-given names are explicitly uncomplimentary, translating as "I am dead" or "I am ugly," in order to avoid the jealousy of ancestral spirits who might wish to take a child that is especially healthy or attractive.

The BEST order is:

A. III, I, II, V, IV B. III, IV, II, I, V C. IV, III, I, II, V D. IV, V, III, I, II

19. I. Though uncertain of the definite reasons for this behavior, scientists believe the birds digest the clay in order to counteract toxins contained in the seeds of certain fruits that are eaten by macaws. 19.____

II. For example, all macaws flock to riverbanks at certain times of the year to eat the clay that is found in river mud.

III. The macaws of South America are not only among the largest and most beautifully colored of the world's flying birds, but they are also one of the smartest.

IV. It is believed that macaws are forced to resort to these toxic fruits during the dry season, when foods are more scarce.

V. The macaw's intelligence has led to intense study by scientists, who have discovered some macaw behaviors that have not yet been explained.

The BEST order is:

A. III, IV, I, II, V B. III, V, II, I, IV C. V, II, I, IV, III D. IV, I, II, III, V

20. I. Although Maggie Kuhn has since passed away, the Gray Panthers are still waging a campaign to reinstate the historical view of the elderly as people whose experience allows them to make their greatest contribution in their later years. 20.____

II. In 1972, an elderly woman named Maggie Kuhn responded to this sort of treatment by forming a group called the Gray Panthers, an organization of both old and young adults with the common goal of creating change.

III. This attitude is reflected strongly in the way elderly people are treated by our society; many are forced into early retirement, or are placed in rest homes in which they are isolated from their communities.

IV. Unlike most other cultures around the world, Americans tend to look upon old age with a sense of dread and sadness.

V. Kuhn believed that when the elderly are forced to withdraw into lives that lack purpose, society loses one of its greatest resources: people who have a lifetime of experience and wisdom to offer their communities.

The BEST order is:

A. IV, III, II, V, I B. IV, II, I, III, V C. II, IV, III, V, I D. II, I, IV, III, V

21. I. The current theory among most anthropologists is that humans evolved from apes who lived in trees near the grasslands of Africa. 21.____

II. Still, some anthropologists insist that such an invention was necessary for the survival of early humans, and point to the Kung Bushmen of central Africa as a society in which the sling is still used in this way.

III. Two of these inventions—fire, and weapons such as spears and clubs—were obvious defenses against predators, and there is archaeological evidence to support the theory of their use.

IV. Once people had evolved enough to leave the safety of trees and walk upright, they needed the protection of several inventions in order to survive.
V. But another invention, a feather or fiber sling that allowed mothers to carry children while leaving their hands free to gather roots or berries, would certainly have decomposed and left behind no trace of itself.
The BEST order is:
A. I, II, III, V, IV B. IV, I, II, III, V C. I, IV, III, V, II D. IV, III, V, II, I

22. I. The person holding the bird should keep it in hot water up to its neck, and the person cleaning should work a mild solution of dishwashing liquid into the bird's plumage, paying close attention to the head and neck. 22.____
II. When rinsing the bird, after all the oil has been removed, the running water should be directed against the lay of its feathers, until water begins to bead off the surface of the feathers—a sign that all the detergent has been rinsed out.
III. If you have rescued a sea bird from an oil spill and want to restore it to clean and normal living, you need a large sink, a constant supply of running hot water (a little over 100ºF), and regular dishwashing liquid.
IV. This cleaning with detergent solution should be repeated as many times as it takes to remove all traces of oil from the bird's feathers, sometime over a period of several days.
V. But before you begin to clean the bird, you must find a partner because cleaning an oiled bird is a two-person job.
The BEST order is:
A. III, I, II, IV, V B. III, V, I, IV, II C. III, I, IV, V, II D. III, IV, V, I, II

23. I. The most difficult time of year for the Tsaatang is the spring calving, when the reindeer leave their wintering ground and rush to their accustomed calving place, without stopping by night or by day. 23.____
II. Reindeer travel in herds, and though some animals are tamed by the Tsaatang for riding or milking, the herds are allowed to roam free.
III. This journey is hard for the Tsaatang, who carry all their possessions with them, but once it's over it proves worthwhile; the Tsaatang can immediately begin to gather milk from reindeer cows who have given birth.
IV. The Tsaatang, a small tribe who live in the far northwest corner of Mongolia, practice a lifestyle that is completely dependent on the reindeer, their main resource for food, clothing, and transport.
V. The people must follow their yearly migrations, living in portable shelters that resemble Native American tepees.
The BEST order is:
A. I, III, II, V, IV B. I, IV, II, V, III C. IV, I, III, V, II D. IV II, V, I, III

24. I. The Romans later improved this system by installing these heated pipe networks throughout walls and ceilings, supplying heat to even the uppermost floors of a building—a system that, to this day, hasn't been much improved. 24.____
II. Air-conditioning, the method by which humans control indoor temperatures, was practiced much earlier than most people think.

III. The earliest heating devices other than open fires were used in 350 B.C. by the ancient Greeks, who directed air that had been heated by underground fires into baked clay pipes that ran under the floor.
IV. Ironically, the first successful cooling system, patented in England in 1831, used fire as its main energy source—fires were lit in the attic of a building, creating an updraft of air that drew cool air into the building through ducts that had underground openings near the river Thames.
V. Cooling buildings was more of a challenge, and wasn't attempted until 1500: a water-based system, designed by Leonardo da Vinci, does not appear to have been successful, since it was never used again.

The BEST order is:

A. III, V, IV, I, II B. III, I, II, V, IV C. II, III, I, V, IV D. IV, II, III, I, V

25. I. Cold, dry air from Canada passes over the Rocky Mountains and sweeps down onto the plains, where it collides with warm, moist air from the waters of the Gulf of Mexico, and when the two air masses meet, the resulting disturbance sometimes forms a violent funnel cloud that strikes the earth and destroys virtually everything in its path. 25.____
II. Hurricanes, storms which are generally not this violent and last much longer, are usually given names by meteorologists, but this tradition cannot be applied to tornados, which have a life span measured in minutes and disappear in the same way as they are born—unnamed.
III. A tornado funnel forms rotating columns of air whose speed reaches three hundred miles an hour—a speed that can only be estimated, because no wind-measuring devices in the direct path of a storm have ever survived.
IV. The natural phenomena known as tornados occur primarily over the Midwestern grasslands of the United States.
V. It is here, meteorologists tell us, that conditions for the formation of tornados are sometimes perfect during the spring months.

The BEST order is:

A. II IV, V, I, III B. II, III, I, V, IV C. IV, V, I, III, II D. IV, III, I, V, II

KEY (CORRECT ANSWERS)

1. C
2. C
3. B
4. A
5. B

6. D
7. C
8. D
9. A
10. C

11. B
12. A
13. D
14. B
15. A

16. D
17. C
18. A
19. B
20. A

21. C
22. B
23. D
24. C
25. C

PREPARING WRITTEN MATERIALS

EXAMINATION SECTION

TEST 1

DIRECTIONS: Each question consists of a sentence which may be classified appropriately under one of the following four categories:
A. Incorrect because of faulty grammar or sentence structure;
B. Incorrect because of faulty punctuation;
C. Incorrect because of faulty capitalization;
D. Correct

Examine each sentence carefully. Then, in the space at the right, indicate the letter preceding the category which is the BEST of the four suggested above. Each incorrect sentence contains only one type of error. Consider a sentence correct if it contains no errors, although there may be other correct ways of expressing the same thought.

1. All the employees, in this office, are over twenty-one years old. 1.____

2. Neither the clerk nor the stenographer was able to explain what had happened. 2.____

3. Mr. Johnson did not know who he would assign to type the order. 3.____

4. Mr. Marshall called her to report for work on Saturday. 4.____

5. He might of arrived on time if the train has not been delayed. 5.____

6. Some employees on the other hand, are required to fill out these forms every month. 6.____

7. The supervisor issued special instructions to his subordinates to prevent their making errors. 7.____

8. Our supervisor Mr. Williams, expects to be promoted in about two weeks. 8.____

9. We were informed that prof. Morgan would attend the conference. 9.____

10. The clerks were assigned to the old building; the stenographers, to the new building. 10.____

11. The supervisor asked Mr. Smith and I to complete the work as quickly as possible. 11.____

12. He said, that before an employee can be permitted to leave, the report must be finished. 12.____

13. A calculator, in addition to the three computers, are needed in the new office. 13.____

14. Having made many errs in her work, the supervisor asked the typist to be more careful. 14.____

15. "If you are given an assignment," he said, "you should begin work on it as quickly as possible." 15.____

16. All the clerks, including those who have been appointed recently are required to work on the new assignment. 16.____

17. The office manager asked each employee to work one Saturday a month. 17.____

18. Neither Mr. Smith nor Mr. Jones was able to finish his assignment on time. 18.____

19. The task of filing these cards is to be divided equally between you and he. 19.____

20. He is an employee whom we consider to be efficient. 20.____

21. I believe that the new employees are not as punctual as us. 21.____

22. The employees, working in this office, are to be congratulated for their work. 22.____

23. The delay in preparing the report was caused, in his opinion, by the lack of proper supervision and coordination. 23.____

24. John Jones accidentally pushed the wrong button and then all the lights went out. 24.____

25. The investigator ought to of had the witness sign the statement. 25.____

KEY (CORRECT ANSWERS)

1.	B	11.	A
2.	D	12.	B
3.	A	13.	A
4.	C	14.	A
5.	A	15.	D
6.	B	16.	B
7.	D	17.	C
8.	B	18.	D
9.	C	19.	A
10.	D	20.	D

21. A
22. B
23. D
24. D
25. A

TEST 2

Questions 1-10.

DIRECTIONS: Each of the following sentences may be classified under one of the following four options:

A. Faulty; contains an error in grammar only
B. Faulty; contains an error in spelling only
C. Faulty; contains an error in grammar and an error in spelling
D. Correct; contains no error in grammar or in spelling

Examine each sentence carefully to determine under which of the above four options it is BEST classified. Then, in the space at the right, write the letter preceding the option which is the best of the four listed above.

1. A recognized principle of good management is that an assignment should be given to whomever is best qualified to carry it out. 1.____

2. He considered it a privilege to be allowed to review and summarize the technical reports issued annually by your agency. 2.____

3. Because the warehouse was in an inaccessible location, deliveries of electric fixtures from the warehouse were made only in large lots. 3.____

4. Having requisitioned the office supplies, Miss Brown returned to her desk and resumed the computation of petty cash disbursements. 4.____

5. One of the advantages of this chemical solution is that records treated with it are not inflamable. 5.____

6. The complaint of this employee, in addition to the complaints of the other employees, were submitted to the grievance committee. 6.____

7. A study of the duties and responsibilities of each of the various categories of employees was conducted by an unprejudiced classification analyst. 7.____

8. Ties of friendship with this subordinate compels him to withold the censure that the subordinate deserves. 8.____

9. Neither of the agencies are affected by the decision to institute a program for rehabilitating physically handi-caped men and women. 9.____

10. The chairman stated that the argument between you and he was creating an intolerable situation. 10.____

Questions 11-25.

DIRECTIONS: Each of the following sentences may be classified under one of the following four options:

A. Correct
B. Sentence contains an error in spelling
C. Sentence contains an error in grammar
D. Sentence contains errors in both grammar and spelling.

11. He reported that he had had a really good time during his vacation although the farm was located in a very inaccessible portion of the country. 11.____

12. It looks to me like he has been fasinated by that beautiful painting. 12.____

13. We have permitted these kind of pencils to accumulate on our shelves, knowing we can sell them at a profit of five cents apiece any time we choose. 13.____

14. Believing that you will want an unexagerated estimate of the amount of business we can expect, I have made every effort to secure accurate figures. 14.____

15. Each and every man, woman and child in that untrammeled wilderness carry guns for protection against the wild animals. 15.____

16. Although this process is different than the one to which he is accustomed, a good chemist will have no trouble. 16.____

17. Insensible to the fuming and fretting going on about him, the engineer continued to drive the mammoth dynamo to its utmost capacity. 17.____

18. Everyone had studied his lesson carefully and was consequently well prepared when the instructor began to discuss the fourth dimention. 18.____

19. I learned Johnny six new arithmetic problems this afternoon. 19.____

20. Athletics is urged by our most prominent citizens as the pursuit which will enable the younger generation to achieve that ideal of education, a sound mind in a sound body. 20.____

21. He did not see whoever was at the door very clearly but thinks it was the city tax appraiser. 21.____

22. He could not scarsely believe that his theories had been substantiated in this convincing fashion. 22.____

23. Although you have displayed great ingenuity in carrying out your assignments, the choice for the position still lies among Brown and Smith. 23.____

24. If they had have pleaded at the time that Smith was an accessory to the crime, it would have lessened the punishment. 24.____

25. It has proven indispensible in his compilation of the facts in the matter. 25.____

KEY (CORRECT ANSWERS)

1.	A	11.	A
2.	D	12.	D
3.	B	13.	C
4.	D	14.	B
5.	B	15.	D
6.	A	16.	C
7.	D	17.	A
8.	C	18.	B
9.	C	19.	C
10.	A	20.	A

21. B
22. D
23. C
24. D
25. B

TEST 3

Questions 1-5.

DIRECTIONS: Questions 1 through 5 consist of sentences which may or may not contain errors in grammar or spelling or both. Sentences which do not contain errors in grammar or spelling or both are to be considered correct, even though there may be other correct ways of expressing the same thought. Examine each sentence carefully. Then, in the space at the right, write the letter of the answer which is the BEST of those suggested below.

A. If the sentence is correct
B. If the sentence contains an error in spelling
C. If the sentence contains an error in grammar
D. If the sentence contains errors in both grammar and spelling.

1. Brown is doing fine although the work is irrevelant to his training. 1.____

2. The conference of sales managers voted to set its adjournment at one o'clock in order to give those present an opportunity to get rid of all merchandise. 2.____

3. He decided that in view of what had taken place at the hotel that he ought to stay and thank the benificent stranger who had rescued him from an embarassing situation. 3.____

4. Since you object to me criticizing your letter, I have no alternative but to consider you a mercenary scoundrel. 4.____

5. I rushed home ahead of schedule so that you will leave me go to the picnic with Mary. 5.____

Questions 6-15.

DIRECTIONS: Some of the following sentences contain an error in spelling, word usage, or sentence structure, or punctuation. Some sentences are correct as they stand although there may be other correct ways of expressing the same thought. All incorrect sentences contain only one error. Mark your answer to each question in the space at the right as follows:

A. If the sentence has an error in spelling
B. If the sentence has an error in punctuation or capitalization
C. If the sentence has an error in word usage or sentence structure
D. If the sentence is correct

6. Because the chairman failed to keep the participants from wandering off into irrelevant discussions, it was impossible to reach a consensus before the meeting was adjourned. 6.____

7. Certain employers have an unwritten rule that any applicant, who is over 55 years of age, is automatically excluded from consideration for any position whatsoever. 7.____

8. If the proposal to build schools in some new apartment buildings were to be accepted by the builders, one of the advantages that could be expected to result would be better communication between teachers and parents of schoolchildren. 8.____

9. In this instance, the manufacturer's violation of the law against deseptive packaging was discernible only to an experienced inspector. 9.____

10. The tenants' anger stemmed from the president's going to Washington to testify without consulting them first. 10.____

11. Did the president of this eminent banking company say; "We intend to hire and train a number of these disadvantaged youths?" 11.____

12. In addition, today's confidential secretary must be knowledgable in many different areas: for example, she must know modern techniques for making travel arrangements for the executive. 12.____

13. To avoid further disruption of work in the offices, the protesters were forbidden from entering the building unless they had special passes. 13.____

14. A valuable secondary result of our training conferences is the opportunities afforded for management to observe the reactions of the participants. 14.____

15. Of the two proposals submitted by the committee, the first one is the best. 15.____

Questions 16-25.

DIRECTIONS: Each of the following sentences may be classified MOST appropriately under one of the following three categories:

A. Faulty because of incorrect grammar
B. Faulty because of incorrect punctuation
C. Correct

Examine each sentence. Then, print the capital letter preceding the BEST choice of the three suggested above. All incorrect sentences contain only one type of error. Consider a sentence correct if it contains none of the types of errors mentioned, even though there may be other ways of expressing the same thought.

16. He sent the notice to the clerk who you hired yesterday. 16.____

17. It must be admitted, however that you were not informed of this change. 17.____

18. Only the employees who have served in this grade for at least two years are eligible for promotion. 18.____

19. The work was divided equally between she and Mary. 19.____

20. He thought that you were not available at that time. 20.____

21. When the messenger returns; please give him this package. 21.____

22. The new secretary prepared, typed, addressed, and delivered, the notices. 22.____

23. Walking into the room, his desk can be seen at the rear. 23.____

24. Although John has worked here longer than she, he produces a smaller amount of work. 24.____

25. She said she could of typed this report yesterday. 25.____

KEY (CORRECT ANSWERS)

1. D
2. A
3. D
4. C
5. C

6. A
7. B
8. D
9. A
10. D

11. B
12. A
13. C
14. D
15. C

16. A
17. B
18. C
19. A
20. C

21. B
22. B
23. A
24. C
25. A

TEST 4

Questions 1-5.

DIRECTIONS: Each of the following sentences may be classified MOST appropriately under one of the following three categories:

A. Faulty because of incorrect grammar
B. Faulty because of incorrect punctuation
C. Correct

Examine each sentence. Then, print the capital letter preceding the BEST choice of the three suggested above. All incorrect sentences contain only one type of error. Consider a sentence correct if it contains none of the types of errors mentioned, even though there may be other ways of expressing the same thought.

1. Neither one of these procedures are adequate for the efficient performance of this task. 1.____

2. The keyboard is the tool of the typist; the cash register, the tool of the cashier. 2.____

3. "The assignment must be completed as soon as possible" said the supervisor. 3.____

4. As you know, office handbooks are issued to all new employees. 4.____

5. Writing a speech is sometimes easier than to deliver it before an audience. 5.____

Questions 6-15.

DIRECTIONS: Each statement given in Questions 6 through 15 contains one of the faults of English usage listed below. For each, choose from the options listed the MAJOR fault contained.

A. The statement is not a complete sentence.
B. The statement contains a word or phrase that is redundant.
C. The statement contains a long, less commonly used word when a shorter, more direct word would be acceptable.
D. The statement contains a colloquial expression that normally is avoided in business writing.

6. The fact that this activity will afford an opportunity to meet your group. 6.____

7. Do you think that the two groups can join together for next month's meeting? 7.____

8. This is one of the most exciting new innovations to be introduced into our college. 8.____

9. We expect to consummate the agenda before the meeting ends tomorrow at noon. 9.____

10. While this seminar room is small in size, we think we can use it. 10.____

11. Do you think you can make a modification in the date of the Budget Committee meeting? 11.____

12. We are cognizant of the problem but we think we can ameliorate the situation. 12.____

13. Shall I call you around three on the day I arrive in the City? 13.____

14. Until such time that we know precisely that the students will be present. 14.____

15. The consensus of opinion of all the members present is reported in the minutes. 15.____

Questions 16-25.

DIRECTIONS: For each of Questions 16 through 25, select from the options given below the MOST applicable choice.

A. The sentence is correct.
B. The sentence contains a spelling error only.
C. The sentence contains an English grammar error only.
D. The sentence contains both a spelling error and an English grammar error.

16. Every person in the group is going to do his share. 16.____

17. The man who we selected is new to this University. 17.____

18. She is the older of the four secretaries on the two staffs that are to be combined. 18.____

19. The decision has to be made between him and I. 19.____

20. One of the volunteers are too young for his complicated task, don't you think? 20.____

21. I think your idea is splindid and it will improve this report considerably. 21.____

22. Do you think this is an exagerated account of the behavior you and me observed this morning? 22.____

23. Our supervisor has a clear idea of excelence. 23.____

24. How many occurences were verified by the observers? 24.____

25. We must complete the typing of the draft of the questionaire by noon tomorrow. 25.____

KEY (CORRECT ANSWERS)

1. A
2. C
3. B
4. C
5. A

6. A
7. B
8. B
9. C
10. B

11. C
12. C
13. D
14. A
15. B

16. A
17. C
18. C
19. C
20. D

21. B
22. D
23. B
24. B
25. B

PREPARING WRITTEN MATERIALS

EXAMINATION SECTION

TEST 1

DIRECTIONS: Each question or incomplete statement is followed by several suggested answers or completions. Select the one that BEST answers the question or completes the statement. *PRINT THE LETTER OF THE CORRECT ANSWER IN THE SPACE AT THE RIGHT.*

Questions 1-25.

DIRECTIONS: Questions 1 through 25 consist of sentences which may or may not be examples of good English usage. Consider grammar, punctuation, spelling, capitalization, awkwardness, etc. Examine each sentence and then choose the correct statement about it from the four choices below it. If the English usage in the sentence given is better than it would be with any of the changes suggested in options B, C, and D, choose option A. Do not choose an option that will change the meaning of the sentence.

1. According to Judge Frank, the grocer's sons found guilty of assault and sentenced last Thursday. 1.____
   A. This is an example of acceptable writing.
   B. A comma should be placed after the word *sentenced.*
   C. The word *were* should be placed after *sons.*
   D. The apostrophe in grocer's should be placed after the *s.*

2. The department heads assistant said that the stenographers should type duplicate copies of all contracts, leases, and bills. 2.____
   A. This is an example of acceptable writing,
   B. A comma should be placed before the word "*contracts.*
   C. An apostrophe should be placed before the *s* in *heads.*
   D. Quotation marks should be placed before the *stenographers* and after *bills.*

3. The lawyers questioned the men to determine who was the true property owner? 3.____
   A. This is an example of acceptable writing.
   B. The phrase *questioned the men* should be changed to *asked the men questions.*
   C. The word *was* should be changed to *were.*
   D. The question mark should be changed to a period.

4. The terms stated in the present contract are more specific than those stated in the previous contract. 4.____
   A. This is an example of acceptable writing,
   B. The word *are* should be changed to *is*.
   C. The word *than* should be changed to *then*.
   D. The word *specific* should be changed to *specified*.

5. Of the few lawyers considered, the one who argued more skillful was chosen for the job. 5.____
   A. This is an example of acceptable writing.
   B. The word *more* should be replaced by the word *most*.
   C. The word *skillful* should be replaced by the word *skillfully*.
   D. The word *chosen* should be replaced by the word *selected*.

6. Each of the states has a court of appeals; some states have circuit courts. 6.____
   A. This is an example of acceptable writing
   B. The semi-colon should be changed to a comma.
   C. The word *has* should be changed to *have*.
   D. The word *some* should be capitalized.

7. The court trial has greatly effected the child's mental condition. 7.____
   A. This is an example of acceptable writing.
   B. The word *effected* should be changed to *affected*.
   C. The word *greatly* should be placed after *effected*.
   D. The apostrophe in *child's* should be placed after the *s*.

8. Last week, the petition signed by all the officers was sent to the Better Business Bureau. 8.____
   A. This is an example of acceptable writing.
   B. The phrase *last week* should be placed after *officers*.
   C. A comma should be placed after *petition*.
   D. The word *was* should be changed to *were*.

9. Mr. Farrell claims that he requested form A-12, and three booklets describing court procedures. 9.____
   A. This is an example of acceptable writing.
   B. The word *that* should be eliminated.
   C. A colon should be placed after *requested*.
   D. The comma after *A-12* should be eliminated.

10. We attended a staff conference on Wednesday the new safety and fire rules were discussed. 10.____
   A. This is an example of acceptable writing.
   B. The words *safety*, *fire*, and *rules* should begin with capital letters.
   C. There should be a comma after the word *Wednesday*.
   D. There should be a period after the word *Wednesday*, and the word *the* should begin with a capital letter.

11. Neither the dictionary or the telephone directory could be found in the office library. 11.____
   A. This is an example of acceptable writing.
   B. The word *or* should be changed to *nor*.
   C. The word *library* should be spelled *libery*.
   D. The word *neither* should be changed to *either*.

12. The report would have been typed correctly if the typist could read the draft. 12.____
   A. This is an example of acceptable writing.
   B. The word *would* should be removed.
   C. The word *have* should be inserted after the word *could*.
   D. The word *correctly* should be changed to *correct*.

13. The supervisor brought the reports and forms to an employees desk. 13.____
   A. This is an example of acceptable writing.
   B. The word *brought* should be changed to *took*.
   C. There should be a comma after the word *reports* and a comma after the word *forms*.
   D. The word *employees* should be spelled *employee's*.

14. It's important for all the office personnel to submit their vacation schedules on time. 14.____
   A. This is an example of acceptable writing.
   B. The word *It's* should be spelled *Its*.
   C. The word *their* should be spelled *they're*.
   D. The word *personnel* should be spelled *personal*.

15. The supervisor wants that all staff members report to the office at 9:00 A.M. 15.____
   A. This is an example of acceptable writing.
   B. The word *that* should be removed and the word *to* should be inserted after the word *members*.
   C. There should be a comma after the word *wants* and a comma after the word *office*.
   D. The word *wants* should be changed to *want* and the word *shall* should be inserted after the word *members*.

16. Every morning the clerk opens the office mail and distributes it. 16.____
   A. This is an example of acceptable writing.
   B. The word *opens* should be changed to *letters*.
   C. The word *mail* should be changed to *letters*.
   D. The word *it* should be changed to *them*.

17. The secretary typed more fast on a desktop computer than on a tablet. 17.____
   A. This is an example of acceptable writing.
   B. The words *more fast* should be changed to *faster*.
   C. There should be a comma after the words *desktop computer*.
   D. The word *than* should be changed to *then*.

18. The typist used an extention cord in order to connect her typewriter to the outlet nearest to her desks. 18.____
    A. This is an example of acceptable writing.
    B. A period should be placed after the word *cord*, and the word *in* should have a capital *I*.
    C. A comma should be placed after the word *typewriter*.
    D. The word *extention* should be spelled *extension*.

19. He would have went to the conference if he had received an invitation. 19.____
    A. This is an example of acceptable writing.
    B. The word *went* should be replaced by the word *gone*.
    C. The word *had* should be replaced by *would have*.
    D. The word *conference* should be spelled *conferance*.

20. In order to make the report neater, he spent many hours rewriting it. 20.____
    A. This is an example of acceptable writing.
    B. The word *more* should be inserted before the word *neater*.
    C. There should be a colon after the word *neater*,
    D. The word *spent* should be changed to *have spent*.

21. His supervisor told him that he should of read the memorandum more carefully. 21.____
    A. This is an example of acceptable writing.
    B. The word *memorandum* should be spelled *memorandom*.
    C. The word *of* should be replaced by the word *have*.
    D. The word *carefully* should be replaced by the word *careful*.

22. It was decided that two separate reports should be written. 22.____
    A. This is an example of acceptable writing.
    B. A comma should be inserted after the word *decided*.
    C. The word *be* should be replaced by the word *been*.
    D. A colon should be inserted after the word *that*.

23. She don't seem to understand that the work must be done as soon as possible. 23.____
    A. This is an example of acceptable writing.
    B. The word *doesn't* should replace the word *don't*.
    C. The word *why* should replace the word *that*.
    D. The word *as* before the word *soon* should be eliminated.

24. He excepted praise from his supervisor for a job well done. 24.____
    A. This is an example of acceptable writing.
    B. The word *excepted* should be spelled *accepted*.
    C. The order of the words *well done* should be changed to *done well*.
    D. There should be a comma after the word *supervisor*.

25. What appears to be intentional errors in grammar occur several times in the passage. 25.____
   A. This is an example of acceptable writing.
   B. The word *occur* should be spelled *occur*.
   C. The word *appears* should be changed to *appear*.
   D. The phrase *several times* should be changed to *from time to time*.

KEY (CORRECT ANSWERS)

1.	C	11.	B
2.	C	12.	C
3.	D	13.	D
4.	A	14.	A
5.	C	15.	B
6.	A	16.	A
7.	B	17.	B
8.	A	18.	D
9.	D	19.	B
10.	D	20.	A

21.	C
22.	A
23.	B
24.	B
25.	C

TEST 2

DIRECTIONS: Each question consists of a sentence which may or may not be an example of good formal English usage. Examine each sentence, considering grammar, punctuation, spelling, capitalization, and awkwardness. Then choose the CORRECT statement about it from the four options below it. If the English usage in the sentence given is better than any of the changes suggested in options B, C, or D, pick option A. Do not pick an option that will change the meaning of the sentence. *PRINT THE LETTER OF THE CORRECT ANSWER IN THE SPACE AT THE RIGHT.*

1. I don't know who could possibly of broken it. 1.____
   A. This is an example of acceptable writing.
   B. The word *who* should be replaced by the word *whom.*
   C. The word *of* should be replaced by the word *have.*
   D. The word *broken* should be replaced by the word *broke.*

2. Telephoning is easier than to write. 2.____
   A. This is an example of acceptable writing.
   B. The word *telephoning* should be spelled *telephoneing.*
   C. The word *than* should be replaced by the word *then.*
   D. The words *to write* should be replaced by the word *writing.*

3. The two operators who have been assigned to these consoles are on vacation. 3.____
   A. This is an example of acceptable writing.
   B. A comma should be placed after the word *operators.*
   C. The word *who* should be replaced by the word *whom.*
   D. The word *are* should be replaced by the word *is.*

4. You were suppose to teach me how to operate a plugboard. 4.____
   A. This is an example of acceptable writing,
   B. The word *were* should be replaced by the word *was.*
   C. The word *suppose* should be replaced by the word *supposed.*
   D. The word *teach* should be replaced by the word *team.*

5. If you had taken my advice; you would have spoken with him. 5.____
   A. This is an example of acceptable writing.
   B. The word *advice* should be spelled *advise.*
   C. The words *had taken* should be replaced by the word *take.*
   D. The semicolon should be changed to a comma.

6. The clerk could have completed the assignment on time if he knows where these materials were located. 6.____
   A. This is an example of acceptable writing.
   B. The word *knows* should be replaced by *had known.*
   C. The word "were" should be replaced by *had been.*
   D. The words *where these materials were located* should be replaced by *the location of these materials.*

7. All employees should be given safety training. Not just those who have accidents. 7.____
   A. This is an example of acceptable writing,
   B. The period after the word *training* should be changed to a colon.
   C. The period after the word *training* should be changed to a semicolon, and the first letter of the word *Not* should be changed to a small *n*.
   D. The period after the word *training* should be changed to a comma, and the first letter of the word *Not* should be changed to a small *n*,

8. This proposal is designed to promote employee awareness of the suggestion program, to encourage employee participation in the program, and to increase the number of suggestions submitted. 8.____
   A. This is an example of acceptable writing.
   B. The word *proposal* should be spelled *proposal*.
   C. The words *to increase the number of suggestions submitted* should be changed to *an increase in the number of suggestions is expected.*
   D. The word *promote* should be changed to *enhance*, and the word *increase* should be changed to *add to.*

9. The introduction of inovative managerial techniques should be preceded by careful analysis of the specific circumstances and conditions in each department. 9.____
   A. This is an example of acceptable writing.
   B. The word *techniques* should be spelled *techneques.*
   C. The word *inovative* should be spelled *innovative.*
   D. A comma should be placed after the word *circumstances* and after the word *conditions.*

10. This occurrence indicates that such criticism embarrasses him. 10.____
    A. This is an example of acceptable writing.
    B. The word *occurrence* should be spelled *occurrence*.
    C. The word *criticism* should be spelled *creticism.*
    D. The word *embarrasses* should be spelled *embarasses.*

11. He can recommend a mechanic whose work is reliable. 11.____
    A. This is an example of acceptable writing.
    B. the word *reliable* should be spelled *relyable.*
    C. The word *whose* should be spelled *who's.*
    D. The word *mechanic* should be spelled *mecanic.*

12. She typed quickly; like someone who had not a moment to lose. 12.____
    A. This is an example of acceptable writing.
    B. The word *not* should be removed.
    C. The semicolon should be changed to a comma.
    D. The word *quickly* should be placed before instead of after the word *typed.*

13. She insisted that she had to much work to do. 13.____
   A. This is an example of acceptable writing.
   B. The word *insisted* should be spelled *insisted.*
   C. The word *to* used in front of *much* should be spelled *too.*
   D. The word *do* should be changed to *be done.*

14. The report, along with the accompanying documents, were submitted for review. 14.____
   A. This is an example of acceptable writing.
   B. The words *were submitted* should be changed to *was submitted.*
   C. The word *accompanying* should be spelled *accompaning.*
   D. The comma after the word *report* should be taken out.

15. If others must use your files, be certain that they understand how the system works, but insist that you do all the filing and refiling. 15.____
   A. This is an example of acceptable writing.
   B. There should be a period after the word *works*, and the word *but* should start a new sentence.
   C. The words *filing* and *refiling* should be spelled *fileing* and *refileing.*
   D. There should be a comma after the word *but.*

16. The appeal was not considered because of its late arrival. 16.____
   A. This is an example of acceptable writing.
   B. The word *its* should be changed to *it's.*
   C. The word *its* should be changed to *the.*
   D. The words *late arrival* should be changed to *arrival late.*

17. The letter must be read carefully to determine under which subject it should be filed. 17.____
   A. This is an example of acceptable writing.
   B. The word *under* should be changed to *at.*
   C. The word *determine* should be spelled *determin.*
   D. The word *carefully* should be spelled *carefully.*

18. He showed potential as an office manager, but he lacked skill in delegating work. 18.____
   A. This is an example of acceptable writing.
   B. The word *delegating* should be spelled *delagating.*
   C. The word *potential* should be spelled *potencial.*
   D. The words *he lacked* should be changed to *was lacking.*

19. His supervisor told him that it would be all right to receive personal mail at the office. 19.____
   A. This is an example of acceptable writing.
   B. The words *all right* should be changed to *alright.*
   C. The word *personal* should be spelled *personel.*
   D. The word *mail* should be changed to *letters.*

20. The report, along with the accompanying documents, were submitted for review. 20.____
   A. This is an example of acceptable writing.
   B. The words *were submitted* should be changed to *was submitted.*
   C. The word *accompanying* should be spelled *accompaning.*
   D. The comma after the word *report* should be taken out.

KEY (CORRECT ANSWERS)

1.	C	11.	A
2.	D	12.	C
3.	A	13.	C
4.	C	14.	B
5.	D	15.	A
6.	B	16.	A
7.	D	17.	D
8.	A	18.	A
9.	C	19.	A
10.	A	20.	B

WRITTEN ENGLISH EXPRESSION
EXAMINATION SECTION
TEST 1

DIRECTIONS: The following questions are designed to test your knowledge of grammar, sentence structure, correct usage, and punctuation. In each group there is one sentence that contains no errors. Select the letter of the CORRECT sentence. *PRINT THE LETTER OF THE CORRECT ANSWER IN THE SPACE AT THE RIGHT.*

1. A. A low ceiling is when the atmospheric conditions make flying inadvisable. 1.____
   B. They couldn't tell who the card was from.
   C. No one but you and I are to help him.
   D. What kind of a teacher would you like to be?
   E. To him fall the duties of foster parent.

2. A. They couldn't tell whom the cable was from. 2.____
   B. We like these better than those kind.
   C. It is a test of you more than I.
   D. The person in charge being him, there can be no change in policy.
   E. Chicago is larger than any city in Illinois.

3. A. Do as we do for the celebration. 3.____
   B. Do either of you care to join us?
   C. A child's food requirements differ from the adult.
   D. A large family including two uncles and four grandparents live at the hotel.
   E. Due to bad weather, the game was postponed.

4. A. If they would have done that they might have succeeded. 4.____
   B. Neither the hot days or the humid nights annoy our Southern visitor.
   C. Some people do not gain favor because they are kind of tactless.
   D. No sooner had the turning point come than a new issue arose.
   E. I wish that I was in Florida now.

5. A. We haven't hardly enough tine. 5.____
   B. Immigration is when people come into a foreign country to live.
   C. After each side gave their version, the affair was over with.
   D. Every one of the cars were tagged by the police.
   E. He either will fail in his attempt or will seek other employment.

6. A. They can't seem to see it when I explain the theory. 6.____
   B. It is difficult to find the genuine signature between all those submitted.
   C. She can't understand why they don't remember who to give the letter to
   D. Every man and woman in America is interested in his tax bill.
   E. Honor as well as profit are to be gained by these studies.

7. A. He arrived safe. 7.____
B. I do not have any faith in John running for office.
C. The musicians began to play tunefully and keeping the proper tempo indicated for the selection.
D. Mary's maid of honor bought the kind of an outfit suitable for an afternoon wedding.
E. If you would have studied the problem carefully you would have found the solution more quickly.

8. A. The new plant is to be electric lighted. 8.____
B. The reason the speaker was offended was that the audience was inattentive.
C. There appears to be conditions that govern his behavior.
D. Either of the men are influential enough to control the situation.
E. The gallery with all its pictures were destroyed.

9. A. If you would have listened more carefully, you would have heard your name called. 9.____
B. Did you inquire if your brother were returning soon?
C. We are likely to have rain before nightfall.
D. Let's you and I plan next summer's vacation together.
E. The man whom I thought was my friend deceived me.

10. A. There's a man and his wife waiting for the doctor since early this morning. 10.____
B. The owner of the market with his assistants is applying the most modern principles of merchandise display.
C. Every one of the players on both of the competing teams were awarded a gold watch.
D. The records of the trial indicated that, even before attaining manhood, the murderer's parents were both dead.
E. We had no sooner entered the room when the bell rang.

11. A. Why don't you start the play like I told you? 11.____
B. I didn't find the construction of the second house much different from that of the first one I saw.
C. "When", inquired the child, "Will we begin celebrating my birthday?"
D. There isn't nothing left to do but not to see him anymore.
E. There goes the last piece of cake and the last spoonful of ice cream.

12. A. The child could find neither the shoe or the stocking. 12.____
B. The musicians began to play tunefully and keeping the proper tempo indicated for the selection.
C. The amount of curious people who turned out for Opening Night was beyond calculation.
D. I fully expected that the children would be at their desks and to find them ready to begin work,
E. "Indeed," mused the poll-taker, "the winning candidate is much happier than I."

13. A. Just as you said, I find myself gaining weight. 13.____
B. A teacher should leave the capable pupils engage in creative activities.
C. The teacher spoke continually during the entire lesson, which, of course, was poor procedure.
D. We saw him steal into the room, pick up the letter, and tear it's contents to shreds.
E. It is so dark that I can't hardly see.

14. A. The new schedule of working hours and rates was satis factory to both employees and employer. 14.____
B. Many common people feel keenly about the injustices of Power Politics.
C. Mr. and Mrs. Burns felt that their grandchild was awfully cute when he waved good-bye.
D. The tallest of the twins was also the most intelligent,
E. Please come here and try and help me finish this piece of work.

15. A. My younger brother insists that he is as tall as me. 15.____
B. Suffering from a severe headache all day, one dose of the prescribed medicine relieved me,
C. "Please let my brothers and I help you with your packages," said Frank to Mrs. Powers.
D. Every one of the rooms we visited had displays of pupils' work in them.
E. Do you intend bringing most of the refreshments yourself?

16. A. The telephone linesmen, working steadily at their task during the severe storm, the telephones soon began to ring again. 16.____
B. Meat, as well as fruits and vegetables, is considered essential to a proper diet.
C. He looked like a real good boxer that night in the ring.
D. The man has worked steadily for fifteen years before he decided to open his own business.
E. The winters were hard and dreary, nothing could live without shelter.

17. A. No one can foretell when I will have another opportunity like that one again. 17.____
B. The last group of paintings shown appear really to have captured the most modern techniques,
C. We searched high and low, both in the attic and cellar, but were unsuccessful in locating mementos.
D. None of the guests was able to give the rules of the game accurately.
E. When you go to the library tomorrow, please bring this book to the librarian in the reference room.

18. A. After the debate, every one of the speakers realized that, given another chance, he could have done better. 18.____
B. The reason given by the physician for the patient's trouble was because of his poor eating habits.
C. The fog was so thick that the driver couldn't hardly see more than ten feet ahead.
D. I suggest that you present the medal to who you think best.
E. I don't approve of him going along.

19. A. A decision made by a man without much deliberation is sometimes no different than a slow one. 19.____
B. By the time Mr. Brown's son will graduate Dental School, he will be twenty-six years of age.
C. Who did you predict would win the election?
D. The auctioneer had less stamps to sell this year than last year.
E. Being that he is occupied, I shall not disturb him.

20. A. Having pranced into the arena with little grace and unsteady hoof for the jumps ahead, the driver reined his horse. 20.____
B. Once the dog wagged it's tail, you knew it was a friendly animal.
C. Like a great many artists, his life was a tragedy.
D. When asked to choose corn, cabbage, or potatoes, the diner selected the latter.
E. The record of the winning team was among the most noteworthy of the season.

21. A. The maid wasn't so small that she couldn't reach the top window for cleaning. 21.____
B. Many people feel that powdered coffee produces a really good flavor.
C. Would you mind me trying that coat on for size?
D. This chair looks much different than the chair we selected in the store.
E. I wish that he would have talked to me about the lesson before he presented it.

22. A. After trying unsuccessfully to land a job in the city, Will located in the country on a farm. 22.____
B. On the last attempt, the pole-vaulter came nearly to getting hurt.
C. The observance of Armistice Day throughout the world offers an opportunity to reflect on the horrors of war.
D. Outside of the mistakes in spelling, the child's letter was a very good one.
E. The annual income of New York is far greater than Florida.

23. A. Scissors is always dangerous for a child to handle. 23.____
B. I assure you that I will not yield to pressure to sell my interest.
C. Ask him if he has recall of the incident which took place at our first meeting.
D. The manager felt like as not to order his usher-captain to surrender his uniform,
E. Everyone on the boat said their prayers when the storm grew worse.

24. A. The mother of the bride climaxed the occasion by exclaiming, "I want my children should be happy forever." 24.____
B. We read in the papers where the prospects for peace are improving.
C. "Can I share the cab with you?" was frequently heard during the period of gas rationing.
D. The man was enamored with his friend"s sister.
E. Had the police suspected the ruse, they would have taken proper precautions.

25. A. The teacher admonished the other students neither to speak to John, nor should they annoy him. 25.____
B. Fortunately we had been told that there was but one service station in that area.
C. An usher seldom rises above a theatre manager.
D. The epic, "Gone With the Wind," is supposed to have taken place during the Civil War Era.
E. Now that she has been graduated she should be encouraged to make her own choice as to the career she is to follow.

KEY (CORRECT ANSWERS)

1. E
2. A
3. A
4. D
5. E
6. D
7. A
8. B
9. C
10. B
11. B
12. E
13. A
14. A
15. E
16. B
17. D
18. A
19. C
20. E
21. B
22. C
23. B
24. E
25. B

TEST 2

DIRECTIONS: The following questions are designed to test your knowledge of grammar, sentence structure, correct usage, and punctuation. In each group, there is one sentence that contains no errors. Select the letter of the CORRECT sentence. *PRINT THE LETTER OF THE CORRECT ANSWER IN THE SPACE AT THE RIGHT.*

1. A. Shall you be at home, let us say, on Sunday at two o'clock? 1.____
   B. We see Mr. Lewis take his car out of the garage daily, newly polished always.
   C. We have no place to keep our rubbers, only in the hall closet.
   D. Isn't it true what you told me about the best way to prepare for an examination?
   E. Mathematics is among my favorite subjects.

2. A. The host thought the guests were of the hungry kinds so he prepared much food. 2.____
   B. The museum is often visited by students who are fond of early inventions, and especially patent attorneys.
   C. I rose to nominate the man who most of us felt was the most diligent worker in the group.
   D. The child was sent to the store to purchase a bottle of milk, and brought home fresh rolls, too.
   E. Hidden away in the closet, I found the long-lost purse.

3. A. The garden tool was sent to be sharpened, and a new handle to be put on. 3.____
   B. At the end of her vacation, Joan came home with little money, but which systematic thrift soon overcame.
   C. We people have opportunities to show the rest of the world how real democracy functions.
   D. The guide paddled along, then fell in a reverie which he related the history of the region.
   E. No sooner had the curtain dropped when the audience shouted its approval in chorus.

4. A. The data you need is to be made available shortly. 4.____
   B. The first few strokes of the brush were enough to convince me that Tom could paint much better than me.
   C. We inquired if we could see the owner of the store, after we waited for one hour.
   D. The highly-strung parent was aggravated by the slightest noise that the baby made.
   E. We should have investigated the cause of the noise by bringing the car to a halt.

5. A. The police, investigating the crime, were successful in discovering only one possibly valuable clue. 5.____
   B. Due to an unexpected change in plans, the violin soloist did not perform.
   C. Besides being awarded a Bachelor's degree at college, the scientist has since received many honorary degrees.
   D. The data offered in advance of the recent Presidential election seems to have possessed elements of inaccuracy.
   E. I don't believe your the only one who has been asked to come here.

6. A. I don't quite see that I will be able to completely finish the job in time. 6.____
   B. By my statement, I infer that you are guilty of the offense as charged.
   C. Wasn't it strange that they wouldn't let no one see the body?
   D. I hope that this is the kind of rolls you requested me to buy.
   E. The storekeeper distributed cigars as bonuses between his many customers.

7. A. He said he preferred the climate of Florida to California. 7.____
   B. Because of the excessive heat, a great amount of fruit juice was drunk by the guests.
   C. This week's dramatic presentation was neither as lively nor as entertaining as last week.
   D. The fashion expert believed that no one could develop new creations more successfully than him.
   E. A collection of Dicken's works is a "must" for every library.

8. A. There was such a large amount of books on the floor that I couldn't find a place for my rocking chair. 8.____
   B. Walking up the rickety stairs, the bottle slipped from his hands and smashed.
   C. The reason they granted his request was because he had a good record.
   D. Little Tommy was proud that the teacher always asked him to bring messages to the office.
   E. That kind of orange is grown only in Florida.

9. A. The new mayor is a resident of this city for thirty years. 9.____
   B. Do you mean to imply that had he not missed that shot he would have won?
   C. Next term I shall be studying French and history.
   D. I read in last night's paper where the sales tax is going to be abolished.
   E. In order to prevent breakage, she placed a sheet of paper between each of the plates when she packed them.

10. A. To have children vie against one another is psychologically unsound. 10.____
    B. Would anyone else care to discuss his baby?
    C. He was interested and aware of the problem.
    D. I sure would like to discover if he is motivating the lesson properly.
    E. The cloth was first lain on a flat surface; then it was pressed with a hot iron.

11. A. She graduated Barnard College twenty-five years ago. 11.____
    B. He studied the violin since he was seven.
    C. She is not so diligent a researcher as her classmate.
    D. He discovered that the new data corresponds with the facts disclosed by Werner.
    E. How could he enjoy the television program; the dog was barking and the baby was crying.

12. A. You have three alternatives: law, dentistry, or teaching. 12.____
    B. If I would have worked harder, I would have accomplished my purpose.
    C. He affected a rapid change of pace and his opponents were outdistanced.
    D. He looked prosperous, although he had been unemployed for a year.
    E. The engine not only furnishes power but light and heat as well.

13. A. The children shared one anothers toys and seemed quite happy. 13.___
B. They lay in the sun for many hours, getting tanned.
C. The reproduction arrived, and had been hung in the living room.
D. First begin by calling the roll.
E. Tell me where you hid it; no one shall ever find it.

14. A. Deliver these things to whomever arrives first. 14.___
B. Everybody but she and me is going to the conference.
C. If the number of patrons is small, we can serve them.
D. When each of the contestants find their book, the debate may begin.
E. Some people, farmers in particular, lament the substitution of butter by margarine.

15. A. After his illness, he stood in the country three weeks. 15.___
B. If you wish to effect a change, submit your suggestions.
C. It is silly to leave children play with knives.
D. Play a trick on her by spilling water down her neck.
E. There was such a crowd of people at the crossing we couldn't hardly get on the bus.

16. A. This is a time when all of us must show our faith and devotion to our country. 16.___
B. Either you or I are certain to be elected president of the new club.
C. The interpellation of the Minister of Finance forced him to explain his policies.
D. After hoisting the anchor and removing the binnacle, the ship was ready to set sail.
E. Please bring me a drink of cold water from the refrigerator.

17. A. Mistakes in English, when due to carelessness or haste, can easily be rectified. 17.___
B. Mr. Jones is one of those persons who will try to keep a promise and usually does.
C. Being very disturbed by what he had heard, Fred decided to postpone his decision.
D. There is a telephone at the other end of the corridor which is constantly in use.
E. In his teaching, he always kept the childrens' interests and needs in mind.

18. A. The lazy pupil, of course, will tend to write the minimum amount of words acceptable. 18.___
B. His success as a political leader consisted mainly of his ability to utter platitudes in a firm and convincing manner.
C. To be cognizant of current affairs, a person must not only read newspapers and magazines but also recent books by recognized authorities.
D. Although we intended to have gone fishing, the sudden outbreak of a storm caused us to change our plans.
E. It is the colleges that must take the responsibility for encouraging greater flexibility in the high-school curriculum.

19. A. "I am sorry," he said, "but John's answer was 'No'." 19.____
B. A spirited argument followed between those who favored and opposed Marie's expulsion from the club.
C. Whether a forward child should be humored or punished often depends upon the circumstances.
D. Excessive alcoholism is certainly not conducive with efficient performance of one's work.
E. Stroking his beard thoughtfully, an idea suddenly came to him.

20. A. "Take care, my children," he said sadly, "lest you not be deceived." 20.____
B. Those continuous telephone calls are preventing Betty from completing her homework.
C. They dug deep into the earth at the spot indicated on the map, but they found nothing.
D. We petted and cozened the little girl until she finally stopped weeping.
E. There was, in the mail, an inquiry for a house by a young couple with two or three bedrooms.

21. A. Please fill in the required information on the application form and return same by April 15. 21.____
B. Tom was sitting there idly, watching the clouds scud across the sky.
C. We started for home so that our parents would not suspect that anything out of the ordinary took place.
D. The sudden abatement from the storm enabled the ladies to resume their journey.
E. Each of the twelve members were agreed that the accused man was innocent.

22. A. The number of gifted students not continuing their education beyond secondary school present a nationwide problem. 22.____
B. A man's animadversions against those he considers his enemies are usually reflections of his own inadequacies.
C. The alembic of his fevered imagination produced some of the greatest romantic poetry of his era.
D. The first case of smallpox dates back more than 3000 years and has gone unchecked until recently.
E. He promised to go irregardless of the rain or snow.

23. A. The child picked up several of the coracles, which he had seen glittering in the sand, and brought them to his mother. 23.____
B. He muttered in dejected tones – and no one contradicted him – "We have failed."
C. A girl whom I believed to be she waved cheerily to me from a passing automobile.
D. We discovered that she was a former resident of our own neighborhood who eloped some years ago with a milkman.
E. It looks now like he will not be promoted after all.

24. A. Mary is the kind of a person on whom you can depend in any emergency. 24.____
B. I am sure that either applicant can fill the job you offer competently and efficiently.
C. Although we searched the entire room, the scissors was not to be found.
D. Being that you are here, we can proceed with the discussion.
E. In spite of our warning whistle, the huge ship continued to sail athwart our course.

25. A. The salaries earned by college graduates vary as much if not more than those earned by high school graduates. 25.____
B. The apothegms that he felt to be so witty were all too often either trite or platitudinous.
C. She read the letter carefully, took out one of the pages, and tore it into small pieces.
D. A young man, who hopes to succeed, must be diligent in his work and alert to his opportunities.
E. No one should plan a long journey for pleasure in these days.

KEY (CORRECT ANSWERS)

1. A
2. C
3. C
4. E
5. A

6. D
7. B
8. E
9. B
10. B

11. C
12. D
13. E
14. C
15. B

16. C
17. A
18. E
19. C
20. C

21. B
22. C
23. B
24. E
25. B

www.ingramcontent.com/pod-product-compliance
Lightning Source LLC
Chambersburg PA
CBHW080322020526
44117CB00035B/2598
9781799347675